RULES ARE NOT ENOUGH
NOT ENOUGH

The art of governance in
the real world

About the author

Rupert Merson is both a chartered accountant and a fellow of the Chartered Institute of Personnel and Development. He was a partner in BDO LLP for 15 years, where he advised organisations of all shapes, sizes and nationalities on 'the problems that arise in the gap between accountancy and human resources'. Rupert now leads his own consulting practice. He has advised companies on governance issues in the UK, Europe and the Middle East. Since 2001 he has been on the faculty of London Business School, where he teaches MBA electives on Managing Growth and New Venture Development. He has also delivered an MBA elective on New Business Ventures at INSEAD in France. He has written four previous books on senior roles in owner-managed businesses: *Owners*, *Managing Directors*, *Finance Directors* and *Non-executive Directors*, all published by Profile Books.

Rupert read English Language and Literature at New College, Oxford, from where he took a first and a university prize. On the side he plays the organ and conducts a choir. He is joint managing director of an establishment in South London that includes four children and a cat.

RULES ARE NOT ENOUGH

The art of governance in the real world

Rupert Merson

PROFILE BOOKS

First published in Great Britain in 2010 by
PROFILE BOOKS LTD
3a Exmouth House
Pine Street
London EC1R 0JH
www.profilebooks.com
in association with BDO LLP
www.bdo.co.uk

A CIP catalogue record for this book is available from the British Library.

ISBN 978 1 84668 091 5

Text design by Sue Lamble
Typeset in Stone by MacGuru Ltd
info@macguru.org.uk
Printed and bound in Britain by
Clays, Bungay, Suffolk

While care has been taken to ensure the accuracy of the contents of
this book, it is intended to provide general guidance only and does not
constitute professional advice.

The paper this book is printed on is certified by the © 1996 Forest
Stewardship Council A.C. (FSC). It is ancient-forest friendly. The printer
holds FSC chain of custody SGS-COC-2061

FSC
Mixed Sources
Product group from well-managed
forests and other controlled sources

Cert no. SGS-COC-2061
www.fsc.org
© 1996 Forest Stewardship Council

To Hazel Brazier
who always knew that rules were not enough

Contents

1 This book – and the usefulness of governance

'I do not care if it was within the rules – it is wrong.'

David Cameron, on MPs' expense claims, May 2009

Governance is receiving a lot of attention at the moment. It usually does when times are bad. In the depths of every recession and after every corporate collapse there is a determination to learn the lesson this time. Despite enquiries and reviews following the company failures in the early 1990s, and then again in the wake of the collapse of Enron, corporate governance is again in the spotlight. Notwithstanding a thorough review of company legislation and the resulting 2006 Companies Act, the foundations of corporate governance are still under scrutiny and the usual questions still being raised. What is the role of a director? Should there be more, less or better regulation? What about the role of non-executives – where were they when we needed them most? How should the remuneration of executives be set? How should a board of directors be structured – the unitary model that to date has found favour among regulators in the UK or the dual supervisory and executive model favoured on the Continent? Should the roles of chairman and CEO be separate? To whom should directors be accountable – the board, the company, the shareholders, stakeholders in general? How should executives be configured and then policed?

The fever of anxiety that has swept the corporate world has affected other spheres of activity as well. The expenses scandal that consumed the Houses of Parliament in early 2009 is essentially a governance scandal, and although the language is different it begs many of the same questions we have just asked. What is the role of the Leader of the House of Commons and how effectively has it been discharged? Should MPs be responsible for determining their own remuneration? What about MPs' expense claims – to what extent should claims be regulated and policed, and how should they be settled?

Just a summary consideration of these issues shows how difficult it can be to answer governance questions. In May 2009 Prime Minister Gordon Brown announced that he was going to introduce a new code of conduct for MPs. Yet it has not been just for the lack of a rulebook that MPs have got themselves into such a mess. As Conservative Party leader David Cameron notes in the quotation that heads this introductory chapter, you can stick to the rules but still be in the wrong. A new code or rulebook might just create further opportunities for individuals to find ways of achieving what they want while still being able to claim they have kept to the rules. Maybe the rules do need changing again, but governance evidently has to be about more than rules, their policing and whether or not individuals have complied with them.

This book wrestles with these questions. It is not a textbook; there are lots of textbooks on governance, some of which I list in the bibliography. Nor is it a manual aimed at those executives or those of their advisers whose interest in corporate governance is only driven by a determination to tick the right boxes – though I hope, of course, both these constituencies find it of interest. This book is aimed at business owners, managers and leaders who are looking for ways of ensuring their businesses have the best possible chance of success, who are facing up to the questions raised above, and who are wondering whether there might be something in this governance thing that might actually help them. This is a book for real managers who are trying to deal with real issues; who are looking to the thinking collected under the governance heading as a source of help, rather than as something for them to wriggle through.

Governance – just a necessary evil?

There are a couple of dragons in these opening paragraphs that need slaying. For starters, there is an inference that many assume governance has little to do with management – indeed that corporate governance is likely to get in the way of management; a nuisance that needs to be dealt with, like tax or employment legislation. There are many who feel that corporate governance is a powerful and insidious force wielded by external agencies who do not really have the interests of managers, or their organisations, at heart. To them corporate governance at best is a necessary evil – a price you have to pay if you are a listed company in particular, along with accountancy, legal and 'nominated adviser' or NOMAD fees. When governance is seen only as a cost it adds nothing. But I believe, and argue in this book, that governance, properly framed, has much to offer businesses and those responsible for them and involved in them – owners, managers, financiers, customers, suppliers, government and regulators.

A second inference is that corporate governance is aimed at an important, but in reality very small, group of people; those responsible for the direction of major incorporated organisations (and large ones at that), with diverse groups of

3

shareholders who trade their shares through the vehicle of regulated stock markets such as the London Stock Exchange – a select group running a small number of companies. This is indeed a view accepted by many. In fact, the focus of much corporate governance can seem narrower even than this: the late Sir Derek Higgs, commenting on his draft report on the role of non-executive directors, noted: 'I do not presume that a one-size-fits-all approach to governance is appropriate.' His report was only aimed at large listed companies. 'Smaller listed companies' were specially treated within 2 pages out of a total of 126, and non-listed companies were offered only the 'hope that the Review will be of wider interest and use'. Higgs's narrowness of scope typifies much that is written about governance, and though this is unfair to Higgs, many have inferred that governance has little to offer even the smaller listed company, let alone the owner-managed business or other forms of organisation.

Furthermore, corporate governance is seen as being imposed by external regulators on an unwilling group of business leaders, while those who are lucky enough to find themselves (for the time being at least) exempt, such as smaller companies and private companies, should be thankful. Certainly there are those who have found themselves in positions of responsibility for big companies whose actions and comments have betrayed a belief that governance has little to do with business success. One executive noted in May 2003, after agreeing under pressure to create a special committee of directors to probe some serious governance-related allegations: 'We will do our best to ensure that corporate-governance fanatics do not throw the baby out with the bathwater.'[1] Of corporate governance, the same executive observed: 'like all fads, [it] has its zealots'. A month later, obviously feeling not much better, he complained: 'This corporate governance thing ... is a sideshow. It is just a public relations stunt, really.' The executive quoted here is Conrad Black, whose subsequent track record hardly lends his comments credibility.

Perhaps Conrad Black's views on corporate governance can be discounted. Perhaps indeed he now thinks differently as he passes his time in prison. But other, more reputable senior executives have evidently harboured similar views about governance issues. Lord Young of Graffham, former Secretary of State for Trade and Industry under Margaret Thatcher and ex-Chairman of Cable & Wireless, announced as he was leaving his post of President of the Institute of Directors, that the role of non-executive director, one of the mainstays of most corporate governance regimes, should be done away with altogether. All directors should become full-time and executive, leaving independent scrutiny to shareholders. It was 'dangerous nonsense', he said, to assume that part-time non-executives could know enough about what was going on to spot problems. Lord Young's views were controversial even when he expressed them in 2002. Certainly the Institute of Directors sought to distance itself from them. The incoming president, presumably speaking in an official capacity, said: 'Lord Young is speaking in a personal capacity and his views do not reflect the policy of the Institute'. (Although Lord Young had given up the chairmanship by then, there is some irony that Cable & Wireless's plummeting share price in the autumn of 2002 was accompanied by a chorus of criticism in the newspapers about the role of the non-executives.) Michael Grade, formerly Chairman of the BBC and until recently Executive Chairman of ITV, expressing perhaps a commonly felt bewilderment rather than giving voice to a criticism, noted that a non-executive director was a bit like a bidet – no one knows what it does, but it adds a bit of class.

Notwithstanding the governance scandals at the beginning of the current century, and the flurry of codes, guidelines and regulations both stressing the importance of the non-executive role and seeking to regulate it, questions were asked again as the recession took hold in 2009 in the wake of banking collapses and financial scandals. Giving evidence to MPs on the Treasury Select Committee in January 2009, Peter Chambers, Chief Executive of Legal & General Investment Management, said of banking non-executives: 'One would have to conclude that non-executive directors were not effective in controlling the activities of the executive directors otherwise we would not be where we are now.'[2]

For others, actions seem to speak louder than words about their attitude to some of the key precepts of corporate governance. When Alliance Boots was taken private in 2007, its biggest shareholder, Stefano Pessina, took the role of Executive Chairman, thus slaying a sacred cow of current corporate governance practice (at least in the UK) that the roles of chief executive and chairman should be split. Now that the privately owned Alliance Boots no longer needed to 'comply or explain' as regards the provisions of the Combined Code on Corporate Governance, compliance ceased to matter. Maybe going private did make all the difference. Erstwhile Chief Executive Richard Baker resigned.

Another interpretation of Pessina's action is that there are elements in the governance codes that are unnecessarily rigorous, or that have little to do with the real world of management. Or maybe governance is all about setting a benchmark for management that is above the standard that managers will set when left to their own devices, but deemed necessary nonetheless by those not involved in the business. In either case codes of governance are literally above the worlds of many managers in two senses: governance is on a higher plane than that occupied by the majority of day-to-day managers, and is of relevance to big multi-stakeholder organisations rather than small ones.

I have trouble with all of this. In the pages that follow

I do not restrict the discussion to listed companies, or to big companies – not even just to companies. Indeed, only a small amount of space is given specifically to listed entities; not because they are unimportant – they are already discussed elsewhere – but because the governance agenda has lots to offer many other sorts of organisations as well. Small companies turn into big companies, which eventually on occasion turn back into small ones, or disappear altogether. Private companies take on external finance, and then turn into listed companies, which then merge with others, and then in some instances are taken private again. At the fringes there are organisations, some small, some big, with corporate interests that are difficult to identify separately from those of their owners or managers – sole traders and partnerships, which in turn might pass through various forms of incorporation. At another fringe are those organisations – not-for-profits, charities and social enterprises – whose reasons for existence look very different from those of a listed company. But all of these organisational types are connected, and their interests are interrelated. Taking one organisational type out of this continuum for individual consideration is to presume a stasis where one does not exist. The governance agenda has to apply to the whole continuum, not just one part of it. Governance should not sit above and apart from management, it should be seen as an integral part of it. Nonetheless, almost all the other parts of the continuum contain organisations for which the governance agenda is relevant and useful. In some instances specialist regulators and interest groups have developed codes and guidelines, while in others governance has been an internal matter only.

To take one example. Many of the biggest businesses in the world are family businesses, some of which are listed, many of which are not. Family businesses, big and small, listed and unlisted, have taken governance seriously for a long time; indeed long before the establishment of regulatory authorities such as the Financial Services Authority (FSA) or the Securities and Exchange Commission (SEC). The most ambitious family businesses have long recognised that if they want the business to last and not be damaged by the inevitable stresses that families are subject to, they must take their governance seriously, and many have formalised their governance arrangements. Long before anyone thought of the Combined Code they drafted their own private codes and constitutions, and, often without the help of lawyers, courts, auditors and regulators, have made them work.

What is corporate governance?

Where governance starts and effective, decent management and leadership stops is impossible to determine precisely. Perhaps governance is an attitude, a way of thinking about management and leadership that helps ensure they are effective and decent. Inevitably it includes several elements. Unsurprisingly, therefore, codes of governance stretch to hundreds of pages. When attacking governance or resisting it many individuals tend to sound off about one or two provisions in one or other of the codes, rather than about governance in general, even if it is something called 'corporate governance' that is the butt of their ire. Corporate governance is thus a term used freely about a wide range of structures and processes, but reducing it to a definition is not easy. Some find it easier to define by its absence. The late Boris Fyodorov, Russian politician and economist, used to lament the fact that in Russian he could not find a translation for 'corporate governance'.[3]

Another reason why corporate governance is not easily reducible to a definition is that real business leaders do not need definitions. As with management techniques and approaches in general, governance either works for them or it is not worth bothering about at all. Theorists need definitions, particularly if they subscribe to the idea that management is a science of elements and forces that behave tidily and rationally, and which can be classified and reported statistically. This is not most managers' experience of the reality, but is what happens to governance when it is reduced to a definition, or a code (which often read like sets of definitions). For many, governance only exists in codes, and thus often reads as if it is at least one remove from reality. Maybe, as Justice Potter Stewart noted in a US Supreme Court judgement in 1964 on obscenity, we should stop worrying about defining it: 'I know it when I see it' Justice Potter Stewart said.

Characteristics

But when we see it, what do we see? Even though it can be difficult to define, the following characteristics are typical.

The application of some external standard to internal management processes

Why external? There is an inference that organisations will not be able to set the benchmark at the required level if left to their own devices. An externally imposed standard also allows for a shared frame of reference, facilitating comparability between organisations – important to potential stakeholders, such as sources of finance who are looking to pick and choose where best to put their money. After years of iterations and reformulations spurred on by one governance disaster after another, listed companies now have the Combined Code on Corporate Governance to comply with. Codes set standards, but they also provide mechanisms for sharing good management and leadership practice. It is not just larger listed companies that benefit from the application of external wisdom. Smaller, growing businesses change rapidly, and place pressures on their managers and directors that are if anything more intense than those placed on the directors of listed companies. 'The organisational weaknesses that entrepreneurs confront every day would cause the managers of a mature company to panic' writes Amar Bhide of Columbia Business School.[4] Many such businesses hunger for a bit of structure, and an external reference point or benchmark – something that reassures such a business that its problems are not unique, and that thousands of successful businesses have passed that way before. The more their experience can be shared with the next generation of businesses the fewer mistakes they will make. A code is one way of passing on that experience. There are categories of organisation other than the large listed company that now have governance codes provided for them. In the absence of any tailor-made code for themselves, organisations that do not fall into the category 'larger listed' often start with the Combined Code anyway.

Some way of holding management to account for their actions

Much corporate governance thinking is predicated on the 'agency principle', under which shareholders appoint management as their agents. Theorists argue that it cannot be presumed that agents will act in the interests of their principals (in this case, the shareholders). This approach to governance presumes the need for structures to police management, ensuring they do what they are supposed to do. The presumption is that unless management is held properly to account they will take advantage. Holding management to account is a mindset that all organisations and all management teams can benefit from. Too many directors and managers in smaller businesses take the view that appraisal mechanisms, and structures that oblige individuals to account for their actions, are things that they have been promoted out of. Not true. Such structures are useful in all organisations, even the benign dictatorships that many businesses, owner-managed and listed, seem to find themselves accidentally modelled on. If management is held to account it is more likely that the managers in aggregate will create something that is greater than the sum of their individual talents. Or, perhaps more cynically some argue, will be less likely to put their own self-interest ahead of the interests of the business.

Structures that separate responsibilities, particularly where conflicts of interest might otherwise arise

Many corporate governance mechanisms seek to separate responsibilities, such as the management of the board from management of the company (chairman versus chief executive officer), or giving responsibility for setting management remuneration to independent outsiders rather than to members of management themselves. Conflicts of interest happen everywhere in organisations – from the smallest start-up to the House of Commons – but conflicts of interest are often more pronounced in private businesses than in listed businesses. The CEO of a major family enterprise might find himself as CEO, major shareholder, trustee of a family trust, employee and director – not to mention father of the chief operating officer and husband of the finance director. Good governance is about finding ways of identifying and then managing these conflicts and the risks to the organisation and those involved in it that might otherwise arise, so that once again the business will survive and prosper.

Ensuring the identification and safeguarding of the interests of a wider group of stakeholders

Corporate governance to a degree is about drawing the attention of management to, and obliging them to take account of, the interests of stakeholders they might otherwise rather not worry about. In the listed business, at which most governance thinking has been aimed, that is the shareholders. The interests of this group are different in a private company where the shareholders and managers are often the same people (though their respective interests still need to be separately attended to). But there are other groups too. They include government, suppliers, customers, potential customers, employees and their families. Management has long since ceased to be just about satisfying and protecting the needs of the shareholders, even in a big business. As the world gets more complicated the web of stakeholder interests becomes steadily more tangled, and governance has an ever more important role in helping the organisation address these interests appropriately.

Ensuring independent expertise is introduced into decision-taking processes at the very top of the organisation

In the days before corporate governance was taken seriously in listed companies a non-executive graced the notepaper and knew how to hold a glass of sherry. Nowadays for some the most important ingredient in any governance regime is the nurturing of independent challenge to the executives within a company, and often the most important independent challenge is seen to be that provided by non-executive directors. Indeed, for some, corporate governance is *only* about the role of the non-executive. One of the key responses in the UK to the collapse of Enron and the spate of governance scandals that accompanied it was the inquiry and report of Derek Higgs. His well-received report, we are inclined to forget, was not about corporate governance in the larger listed business, it was about the role of the non-executive.

Non-executives have much to offer the smaller or non-listed business too. A decent non-executive will provide a source of advice that is cheaper than that provided by an adviser; will be able to ensure the business does not lose sight of the bigger picture while the managers are wrestling with the day-to-day; will provide connections to the outside world and to stakeholder groups not otherwise represented in the business; will introduce a greater degree of objectivity into management's decision taking; and will provide a first-line challenge to the thinking of management. Independent challenge is not just the responsibility of the non-executives; it is a function of structure, recruitment, communication and performance management. Is there an organisation anywhere, big or small, listed or privately held, that would not benefit from independent challenge?

Definitions

Each of the above elements will be discussed in more detail in the following pages, but none of them serve as a definition of governance. Although Justice Potter Stewart's line is still tempting, I recognise that it is useful at least to have some shared understanding of what we are talking about. There are many definitions of governance, but the following two formal definitions make for interesting contrasts, and demonstrate the breadth of opinion on governance, what it means and why it matters.

The first – 'The ways in which a firm safeguards the interests of its financiers (investors, lenders, and creditors'[5] – is crisp and simple. The word 'safeguard' implies that there is something that needs to be protected from someone. And it is very clear who needs to be protected – the investors and creditors. Everyone else is deemed to be either not at risk, not worth worrying about or likely to be a member of the guilty party. The definition is less clear about who does the safeguarding. The word 'firm' implies that it is the organisation itself that has this responsibility; though the organisation need not be a company or even an incorporated entity. Presumably an employee of the organisation is responsible for the safeguarding. So governance is something that can be delegated; or something that is done by someone else to you. Whom are the investors being safeguarded from? Indeed are they, their agents or their powers even present in the organisation at all? Governance in this definition is one way. The financial investors are the presumed innocent. Some dark but undefined force is at work in the business with devilish intent. To be fair, the business dictionary that provides this definition describes it as the 'traditional definition'. However, for many governance is a simple, one-dimensional matter of relevance only to organisations with financial stakeholders. For them, the only objective of a company is to make money for its shareholders.

The same dictionary gives us a 'modern' definition: 'The framework of rules and practices by which a board of directors ensures accountability, fairness, and transparency in the firm's relationship with all its stakeholders (financiers, customers, management, employees, government, and the community).'[6] The definition is longer, but much more complex. For starters, it is not just the financiers who are to benefit from the brave new world – a far broader notion of the interested parties is developed. And there is no presumption of innocence offered to the stakeholder community. Governance in this definition does not go just one way; it matters between the organisation and all its stakeholders. There is an implication that all sorts of parties will benefit from governance. The individuals responsible for the governance framework are clearly named – it is the board of directors. And the objectives of decent governance are also named: accountability, fairness and transparency, with 'accountability' implying that personal responsibility matters, and not just on the board; 'fairness' implying the application of certain moral standards;

and 'transparency' introducing the importance of openness, and setting up expectations for standards of communication. It also refers to 'rules' and 'practices' – the former implying standards ('dos and don'ts'), the latter suggesting there should also be room for attitudes, approaches, states of mind and cultures, thus helping to protect against those who think that a rule is just a form of words wrapped around a loophole. Lastly, there is the first word in the definition – 'framework': corporate governance is more than the sum of its parts, and it only becomes the real thing when all the components are incorporated into a framework.

There are, of course, innumerable definitions of corporate governance. Here's another: 'Rules, processes and behaviour that affect the way in which powers are exercised ... particularly as regards openness, participation, accountability, effectiveness and coherence' (European Commission, *European Governance: A White Paper*, 2001). This one openly refers to 'behaviour' as a component and also presents governance as in some way modifying the exercise of 'powers' – which takes us back to Conrad Black, and the constraints he felt on his own powers.

From all the definitions it is possible to isolate some key elements and subject areas, each of which we will discuss in more detail in the chapters that follow:

- **Objectives** – what the organisation is for and how it discharges its objectives.

- **Finance** – where it comes from, the uses to which it is put, and how the interests of the providers of finance are safeguarded.

- **People** – particularly those in positions of influence on the inside of the organisation, and how they should relate to the organisation.

- **Stakeholders** – other people and organisations, often not as close to the organisation as those on the inside but keenly interested nonetheless; their relationship with the organisation, its directors, staff and each other.

- **Rules** – and laws, codes of conduct and guidelines – often drafted to protect investors in listed companies, but increasingly drawn up to protect a broader range of stakeholders in other sorts of organisations. Often drafted by external agencies, but not always.

- **Performance measurement and management** – how systems and structures are used to direct and motivate individuals in the organisation, both with and against their better judgement.

- **Values and culture in the organisation** – intangible elements that influence how individuals within an organisation behave.

- **Transparency** – the availability of information about an organisation and its performance, and the extent to which this information is shared inside the organisation and with the outside world; how much, how often and in what form.

- **Growth and complexity** – recognition that the governance agenda changes as the organisation grows (and grows up) and that one size does not fit all.

- **Structures and power** – who should report to whom in an organisation and how; different ways of structuring management; how power should be exercised and by whom, and what checks and balances should be put on it.

Corporate governance has been described as 'the catch-phrase of the global financial community', which is a sure way of inviting challenges from cynics and naysayers. Yes, it is difficult to define, as we have found out already, and, as we will find out in due course, many of the ways governance works best are intangible rather than concrete, easily measurable ways. And that does not make pinning it down any the easier. But the thinking that comes under the heading of governance provides as good a set of tools and as robust a way of thinking about the responsibilities of management as any. And as we shall discuss before we finish, governance could do much more if only we breathed a bit of life into it and stopped treating it like an empty ceremony or a cold exercise in filling out forms.

2 Objectives

> 'Objectives are not fate; they are direction. They are not commands; they are commitments. They do not determine the future; they are means to mobilize the resources and energies of the business for the making of the future.'
>
> Peter Drucker[7]

Governance is all about how, but before managers and directors worry about how they should give some thought to what. In theory, sorting out an organisation's objectives should be easy, but in practice it is not. In theory, someone once observed, there is no difference between theory and practice, but in practice there is. The problem is that, in attempting to capture practice, theory reduces and simplifies it. Thinking about governance is not exempt from this problem.

The problem starts with objectives. Surely the key to effective governance is a defined set of objectives. Unfortunately, defining objectives is not that simple. For starters, many organisations just happen. Someone is made redundant and they take on a project, which turns into two projects, and then into a business. Very few people, for example, deliberately set out to form a family business. Businesses turn into family businesses when other members of the family get involved. When other people get involved in a business, family or not, they will almost inevitably have their own understanding of what the business is about, and even if they agree on that they will project onto it their own aspirations and expectations – their own personal objectives. The larger the organisation, the more complicated the pattern of objectives, personal and corporate. By the time management attempts for the first time to put together a strategic plan – in effect to establish the direction for the organisation – the objectives have in all likelihood become difficult to pin down.

Many reductionists will cut through all this woolly thinking and pronounce that the objectives of a company, or indeed any business venture, are simple to define in reality (or is it in theory?): it is all about making money, or 'adding value' for the shareholders. In capitalist systems, capitalists put their cash at risk into a venture, and in so doing they turn themselves into shareholders. The venture they create employs management to steer the venture, which then recruits labour, acquires other resource and material, and produces and sells product. If there is a profit to be made, that profit principally returns to the providers of the capital – the shareholders. Because the shareholders are often at one or more removes from the operations of the business itself, systems, structures and safeguards need to be introduced to protect the suppliers of capital from the other stakeholders in the venture, but in particular from the hired managers, who might otherwise take advantage of their privileged positions of power and knowledge to line their own pockets at the expense of the individuals who own the capital. This in essence is the agency theory of management – that management acts as the agent of the shareholders; that the interests of shareholders and managers conflict, and there are costs inherent in aligning them. Corporate governance, under this thinking, is the name given to the systems, structures and safeguards introduced to protect the providers of capital – in particular the providers of equity finance, otherwise known of course as the shareholders.

This approach to governance, which presumes that it is all about protecting shareholders from the machinations of managers, is very common. Al 'Chainsaw' Dunlap, erstwhile CEO of Scott Paper Company, famously claimed: 'Scott should be making money for its shareholders. It is a sin to lose money, a mortal sin.' Dunlap is in educated company. Nobel prize-winning economist Milton Friedman wrote: 'Few trends could so thoroughly undermine the foundations of our free society as the acceptance by corporate officials of a social responsibility other than to make as much money for their stockholders as possible.'[8] The 1998 Hampel Report on corporate governance noted with absolute confidence that: 'The single overriding objective shared by all listed companies, whatever their size or type of business, is the preservation and the greatest practical enhancement over time of their shareholders' investment.'[9] As the recession that started in 2008 deepened, many commentators argued that this version of governance should be turned around: rather than protecting passive shareholders, good governance should encourage and provide mechanisms for shareholders to act as checks and balances on management. 'It is clear we haven't been as effective as we could have been', said Peter Montagnon, Investment Affairs Director at the Association of British Insurers, speaking of institutional investors' inability to curb companies' worst excesses. Sir Peter Viggers, MP for Gosport, implied at a Treasury Select Committee hearing in January 2009 that the current economic crisis had shown that shareholders, as company owners, were 'pretty toothless'. Other institutional shareholder representatives took a slightly different stance: 'Did we engage enough? I think we did' argued Peter Chambers, Chief Executive of Legal & General Investment

Management. 'The question is why we weren't listened to and I do not know the answer to that.'[10]

Whether you take the line that shareholders need protecting from management, or that shareholders should actively involve themselves in controlling management's excesses, there is a presumption that managers will be otherwise inclined not to put shareholders' interests where they should be – first – and that unless appropriately controlled, managers will otherwise act only in their own self-interest. For many the key to the solution of governance involves turning the proposition inside out and aligning the interests of managers with the interests of shareholders. For many this is just a matter of incentives and remuneration: there are plenty of people out there for whom it is *only* money that matters. If it can be guaranteed that managers will manage the business in the interests of shareholders then the interests of the shareholders will be safeguarded, and if the ship starts listing to starboard it will at least be with shareholders and management agreeing that it was only a scratch and not a fatal collision with an iceberg.

Shareholder interests – too simple?

The credit crunch and the ensuing recession have thrown the relationship between the shareholders, the business and the fundamental objectives of the business into the searchlights of those anxious to find out what has gone wrong. As the financial history of the 2008 crash already shows, play fast and loose with the role of finance in the financial system, fail to understand the tensions between the providers of capital and the other stakeholders – and what you get is the credit crunch. In a report published in September 2008, the Association of Chartered Certified Accountants wrote: 'The ACCA believes that underlying much of the credit crunch has been a fundamental failure in corporate governance.' The authors go on to set out a very traditional understanding of the role of corporate governance:

> While the financial institutions involved may have been in compliance with local requirements and codes, they have ignored the key point – good corporate governance is about boards directing and controlling the organisations so they operate in their shareholders' interests. Boards should be answerable to company owners, to account properly for their stewardship and to ensure both sound internal control and the ethical health of the organisations. The use of overly complex financial products, which thwarted effective supervisory control, and the unethical advancement, at the point of sale, of loans to people with little realistic hope of repaying them shows a lack of basic corporate governance.[11]

But it is not just the shareholders who have been dealt a raw deal in the credit crunch. Even the ACCA report quoted above switches halfway through its argument to worrying about the interests of the banks' depositors rather than their shareholders. Bank depositors are a very different sort of financial stakeholder in a business, as we shall discuss later. Indeed, paying too much attention to the money interests, whether shareholder, debtor or creditor, also misses at least some of the point. As the credit crunch is morphing into something arguably much more frightening for 2009 and beyond, more doubt is cast on the role of the shareholder in governance systems. '[I]f the financial system has proved dysfunctional, how far can we rely on the maximisation of shareholder value as the way to guide business?' asks leading economist Martin Wolf.[12] George Soros is one of an increasing number of successful business people who go further and openly disagree with a fixation on shareholders and shareholder value when determining organisational objectives. 'One of the short-comings of American society', he has written, is 'an excessive admiration of success – measured in monetary terms – to the detriment of more intrinsic values.'[13] Jack Welch, former CEO of GE, controversially entered the debate in March 2009, shortly before his old company lost its top credit rating from Standard & Poor's, proposing that: 'On the face of it, shareholder value is the dumbest idea in the world ... Shareholder value is a result, not a strategy ... Your main constituencies are your employees, your customers and your products.'[14]

Much of the most heated discussion about how best to structure approaches to corporate governance lies between these two points of view. My own view is that, in 2009, after yet another wave of company failures, it is surely too simple to argue that corporate governance is just a mechanism for protecting the interests of shareholders, or indeed too simple to think just in terms of 'protection'. The ACCA, as already noted, is right in drawing attention in the case of banks to the depositors and borrowers, many of whom were complaining of harsh treatment as economic circumstances worsened. When governance systems are devised in the interests of one group of individuals it makes sense to talk in terms of protection; but when lots of different types of stakeholders are involved, the concept of protection works less well as a determining characteristic of governance. Indeed, in many businesses it is far too easy to think of the shareholders as a simple, homogeneous group. Many businesses have different classes of shareholder. 'Preferential shareholders' have more in common with debt holders than they do with equity holders, entitled as they are to a fixed dividend and preferential treatment in the event of a liquidation. Some companies, particularly those with sophisticated financial investors, will find they owe money to institutions via a debt instrument that might in some circumstances change into equity. Some businesses, even small ones, have different classes of ordinary shares, each with different rights to voting or return. Yet a further complication is the difference between majority and minority shareholders. A shareholder who owns more than 50 per cent of the shares of a company, a 'majority shareholder', is usually in effect in control of the business, can appoint and remove the directors, and might well be in a position to take advantage of minority shareholders who will not have 'controlling interests', and who will probably be at several further removes away from the business than the majority shareholders – and on occasion treated with unwarranted contempt. Conrad Black, commenting on the minority shareholders in one of his publicly traded enterprises, noted:

> I think what you saw at the annual meeting was …
> impatience. It reminds me of when our children were
> bottle-fed. They were great, healthy, big babies – real
> bruisers. They got to the end of the bottle, and being
> very inexperienced infants, they wanted more. In
> fact there was nothing left in the bottle because the
> contents were inside them. They didn't figure out the
> implications.[15]

Black's attitude to his fellow shareholders ultimately was his undoing, and reminds us that in corporate governance shareholders do not need so much protecting from management as protecting from each other. But in a sense Black is surely right in implying that there is no real reason why he and his fellow shareholders should think anything other than very differently about the businesses in which they shared ownership. Part of the problem when arguing in favour of shareholder activism as a key tool of corporate governance is that in a diversely owned business it can hardly be expected the shareholders will agree with each other in the first place.

Indeed, it is surely too easy even to think of the shareholders as the 'owners' of the business at all. Many shareholders behave, not as if they own the business, but as if they own the money they have invested in it. UK academic Jill Solomon quotes a pension fund director observing:

> There is a weakness in the present system of corporate governance in that responsibility for ownership rests with people who do not want it and are not seeking it. We are investing in shares because they give us a good return and it is coincidental really that they bring with them this responsibility.[16]

This conception of ownership puts shareholders in a very different relation both to each other and to the other stakeholders in the business, and reminds us that, in the complicated modern world – indeed in any world in which people play a part – corporate governance has to be about more than shareholders, and about more than protecting somebody from somebody else.

Partnership objectives

Not all industries generate opportunities that are best satisfied by incorporated entities financed from external sources by remote shareholders. If you need big factories or acres of land you will indeed need large-scale, external finance to make them happen, and this will mean sophisticated capital markets, which in turn will mean incorporated entities – and a particular type of governance. On the other hand there are industries that are suited to the 'owner-managed' model. Not all owner-managed businesses need to be incorporated, and partnerships prevail in several industries. The owner-managed model – partnership in particular – suits industries in which an identification between the owners as individuals and the business of the organisation is important. Such industries tend to be people- rather than asset-intensive. Financiers and factories get in between partners and stop their partnerships happening. Partnerships are conversely peculiarly well suited to knowledge- and people-based businesses. Partnerships address the 'money' problem in different ways from incorporated entities. Many people who have entered industries in which partnerships predominate and who *do not* understand, have assumed that partnerships stand in the same relation to the financial objective as listed companies, that what works for one will suit the other, and have therefore failed to achieve the success they anticipated.

When do partnerships work best? Despite the knowledge management revolution, knowledge businesses' assets continue to be contained between the ears of the principal individuals in the business. A knowledge business will always be based on the personal relationship between an individual adviser and client. A partnership allows the individual to take advantage of scale, and the efficiencies to be derived from working in close proximity with people with complementary skills, but it is still in essence a collection of individuals each with personal relationships with a set of clients. It is significant that many partnerships take their corporate name from the names of the founding partners. The implications of this are often misunderstood, even by partners – and particularly by those in knowledge businesses who have converted their partnerships into incorporated entities, and who thus own share certificates that give their owners the illusion that they own a share of a business that has a value separable from themselves. (Just as there are large partnerships that are in effect run as corporate entities, so there are limited companies that are really still partnerships both at heart and as a matter of commercial reality.)

The matter comes into prominence when a partner,

particularly a founding partner, and one with his or her name on the door, looks to retire. For many such, the prospect of retiring involves a presumption of 'selling' his or her share of the business to the junior partners. Far from being grateful for the opportunity, many junior partners in these circumstances argue that their retiring senior partner is trying to have his cake and eat it. If his personal role has been so considerable, it and its value will leave with him on his retirement. He cannot have it both ways: if he stays he is of value and will earn well; if he goes he will enjoy his retirement, but he will not earn, and will not be rewarded for any 'value' left behind in the business because there will not be much. In essence, therefore, most partnerships are not mechanisms for aggregating value, they are mechanisms for distributing income. The most significant financial capital that is needed in many partnerships is working capital: capital is not needed to finance assets, and surplus financial capital does not find it so easy to earn a return, which again has implications for stakeholders who define their objectives in purely financial terms, and the governance frameworks that surround them.

A case in point in recent years, which illustrates how the partnership model and the relationship between partners, the business and financial stakeholders work, has been the 'consolidator' phenomenon in the accountancy industry. Accountancy is a profitable industry, and financiers have circled it for years wondering how to get a piece of the action – or rather, imagining that there is some action that it would be interesting to get a piece of without having to worry about the perils of owner-management; after all, a partnership that makes money, and that is so inherently scalable (just add more people who are good enough to find new clients) is surely a decent investment proposition. In the past few years financiers have been spinning the wheels on just such a model. The thinking has had a defensible logic: create a business vehicle;

list it on the stock market, and use the money raised to buy up smaller practices around the country. Smaller practices are constrained by lack of resources; membership of a bigger, better-financed entity would give them reach and resource that would otherwise be unobtainable. Furthermore, partnership capital is 'illiquid' – you cannot realise it until you retire, and then you have to find someone willing to finance the withdrawal of your capital. This inevitably will be existing partners or individuals promoted to the partnership to fill your chair, but neither might leap at the opportunity. If you are close to retirement, faced with limited alternatives, you might be tempted by the opportunity to exchange your partnership for cash and marketable shares in a listed entity.

The proposition was attractive enough for a while for a lot of partners with management roles in accountancy practices to be worried for their futures. Numerica, with Levy Gee as its largest member firm and 'base tenant', raised £25 million on the markets and set about acquiring and consolidating smaller practices around the country. But the wheel turned. After a bumpy ride, Numerica itself was swallowed up by a bigger spider, Vantis, another of the consolidators. Tenon, the first of the consolidators onto the London Stock Exchange's Alternative Investment Market (AIM) in March 2000, announced plans to go private again in 2005 – hardly an endorsement of the consolidator model; the plans were subsequently abandoned amid rumours that debt levels were likely to frighten off potential investors. In Australia things have turned out even worse, consolidators Harts Australasia and Stockford collapsed in 2001, and Garrisons Accounting Group was placed in administration in 2003.

Why the difficulties – particularly given the undoubted profitability of the industry as a whole? Some partners, now directors or other types of employee in a listed entity, take the view with hindsight that they were sold a pup. The share options that many of them took (rather than free equity or cash) tied them in rather than offered them realisable value. Even those holding real paper were obliged to watch it decline in value as the consolidators failed to make an impression on new investors. The model was troubled for other reasons. Key decision takers in partnerships often tend to be partners relatively close to retirement; but the partners on whom future business depends are often younger partners, whose earning potential continues to be tied up with the future of the business. Unsurprisingly, some consolidator deals were made by older partners who took the money and looked forward to imminent retirement, but the partners who were left to do the work were left also with the prospect of having to share their returns with financial stakeholders.

Some have defined the problem as old partners retiring unfairly at the expense of junior partners, but it goes further than that, as firms look to recruit junior staff into the bottom of a machine that ultimately depends for its success on its ability to develop senior staff and partners in the future. Why join a practice where the future earnings potential is reduced? We come back to the notion that partnerships of knowledge-management professionals are mechanisms for sharing income, not mechanisms for accumulating value. Another reason, perhaps, why the key decision takers in firms selling to consolidators might have been so minded to sell was that their level of income had not been sufficient to support their expectations. For them, the consolidator model was a ticket out: for the consolidator, the model had the effect of attracting firms that had not been successful enough to realise their ambitions on their own. And they have ended up with senior staff frustrated at sharing business returns with financial stakeholders, and being obliged to comply with governance mechanisms designed for the world of publicly listed corporations.

Of course, the professions are changing, and there are aspects of legal, accounting and other services that can be separated out, productised, externally financed and run using the remote external shareholder and manager model that works in other industries – the growth of legal outsourcing shows this. But in general terms you cannot just take a partnership in a knowledge industry and squeeze it into a management structure driven by the demands of PLCs. The dynamics – certainly the financial dynamics – in knowledge-based professional organisations are different from those in other industries. And the governance structures that suit are likely to take a different form. But governance structures are just as important. The key difference that needs accounting for is that the lever that influences the shape of the governance regime in knowledge-based partnerships is people; in PLCs it is money – money usually contributed by individuals who are remote from the organisations in which they invest, or by institutions which are in effect just a mechanism for removing the ultimate investor – the pensioner or endowment policy holder – even further from the businesses in which they invest. In partnerships, it is people, not money, that talks.

Social enterprises

There are, of course, organisations that are only too proud of the distance they put between their objectives and shareholder interest as a motive. 'Not-for-profit' is another of those labels, like 'chief executive', that have been imported from America. As a title, 'not-for-profit' clearly states that the number one objective of organisations of this sort is not to make money in the form of profit, and by implication it suggests that the chief beneficiaries are not shareholders. Typically the label is used by a range of organisations, including charities (registered or otherwise), social enterprises, clubs, educational establishments, and industrial and provident societies. Many if not most of these organisations do not have shareholders at all, but they certainly have governance issues that need addressing.

Of course, the label 'not-for-profit' is misleading. Such organisations do have to find money from somewhere otherwise they will not exist. Money is the lifeblood of a not-for-profit just as it is the lifeblood of a 'for-profit' corporation. In fact, of course, many not-for-profits do make 'surpluses', and the money they make will be applied to the objects of the enterprise rather than divvied up among shareholders. Perhaps a more realistic title, and the one gaining much currency, is 'social enterprise'. A social enterprise, according to the UK government, is essentially any organisation with primarily social objectives whose surpluses are principally reinvested for that purpose in the business or in the community, rather than being driven by the need to maximise profit for shareholders and owners. As the government itself notes:

> Social enterprises tackle a wide range of social and environmental issues and operate in all parts of the economy. By using business solutions to achieve public good, the Government believes that social enterprises have a distinct and valuable role to play in helping create a strong, sustainable and socially inclusive economy. Social enterprises are diverse. They include local community enterprises, social firms, mutual organisations such as co-operatives, and large-scale organisations operating nationally or internationally. There is no single legal model for social enterprise. They include companies limited by guarantee, industrial and provident societies, and companies limited by shares; some organisations are unincorporated and others are registered charities.[17]

It is a mistake to assume that social enterprises, therefore, are not interested in money – or, indeed, that they do not have much of it. It is also a mistake to assume that such organisations do not have governance needs, albeit those they do have are different from those presumed by the Combined Code.

Social enterprises, though they do indeed include within their number many organisations that survive hand-to-mouth from one week to the next, also include institutions with balance sheets worth many millions. Their financial resources might be the consequence of centuries of stewardship. New College, Oxford was founded in 1379 and benefits from, and is responsible for, the safeguarding of the funds initially left to it by its founder William Wykeham, and supplemented since, and applied to the objectives of a college of academics and students within the framework of the University of Oxford. By contrast, within weeks of the earthquake and the ensuing tsunami centred on Bandeh Aceh in Indonesia on Boxing Day, 2004, charities were overwhelmed with millions of pounds of funds sent from around the world in response to the requests for relief – funds intended to be put at the disposal of the victims of the disaster and those wishing to help them. The victims were numbered in millions, presented thousands of different, often urgent, problems in dozens of different languages and legal jurisdictions. The organisations looking to help were in the hundreds, all with different styles and cultures, aims and objectives, seeking to support, complement and compete with each other. All this presented a governance challenge of the first order, particularly in the way the organisations related to each other – a challenge that would have tested the largest organisation on the planet.

Social enterprises have been increasingly subject to their own forms of specialist governance that suit their own special objectives. Charities in particular are closely regulated by the Charity Commission as to the way in which they manage their finances, and the Charity Commission's guidance and regulatory notes include many on financial stewardship, investment practice, accounting rules and regulations, how charities may deploy their assets, their reserves (too big or too small), the management of commercial subsidiaries and so forth. Social enterprises of all kinds anxiously measure how much of their income they allocate to administration, keen to demonstrate how they maximise the resources they devote to their ultimate objectives.

The ability of charities to conduct commercial activity is one of those matters the regulators take a keen interest in, with important consequences for governance. While charities may trade more or less freely in pursuit of their charitable objectives, there are restrictions on engaging in trades the objective of which is to generate funds for the charity. This might seem to defy common sense, but the real issues are to prevent charities taking advantage of the tax advantages that they benefit from for competitive gain, and putting at risk assets that in reality are supposed to be reserved for charitable activity. That a charity shop might benefit from subsidised rates will occasionally seem a little unfair to the small commercial shop next door.

Charities find ways of working with the regulations in pursuit of their objectives, usually by trading through a subsidiary, which then transfers its profits to its parent charity. Trading subsidiaries may make donations to their parent charity as Gift Aid, so reducing tax liability on the profits of the subsidiary. But running trading subsidiaries involves additional management and costs – and additional governance pressures. There is an inherent tension between the duties of a trustee running the parent charity, and the duties of a director responsible for a subsidiary company established for trading purposes. As one of the Charity Commission's publications makes clear:

> Trustees of charities with one or more trading subsidiaries need to be aware of their responsibilities. In particular they need to remember, in all decisions made in regard to a trading subsidiary, that the interests of the charity are paramount. The interests of a trading subsidiary, its directors, creditors or employees, must all be secondary to those of the charity. This is because the purpose of using a trading subsidiary is to benefit the charity in some way, for example to protect the charity's assets from the risks of trading, or to increase the level of financial return to the charity by saving tax. If the charity's assets are employed or put at risk for the benefit of the subsidiary, or its directors, creditors or employees, then that purpose is frustrated. In such cases, the trustees of the charity may be personally liable for any loss of, or decline in value of, the charity's assets.[18]

The Charity Commission understandably presents the dilemma from the trustees' point of view, but it is a dilemma nonetheless. It is possible to envisage scenarios under which the legitimate concerns of the trustees of the charity clash with the legitimate concerns of the directors of the subsidiary, and there are many instances in which tensions arise in charitable organisations between trustees and subsidiary directors.

The increasing interest in not-for-profits and the blurring of the distinction between organisations that are out to make money and organisations that are created to serve a different purpose have led to an interest in new forms and structures. One such vehicle in the UK is the Community Interest Company (CIC), introduced under the Community Interest Act of 2004. A CIC is a type of limited company, designed for social enterprises that want to use their profits and assets for the public good.

Charities, as noted, are subject to tight regulation, certainly when it comes to commercial activity and the distribution of earnings. In return, charities benefit from tax advantages. A CIC is not allowed to be registered as a charity, though a charity will be allowed to own a CIC, just as a charity can also own a trading subsidiary. A CIC, on the other hand, is much more lightly regulated than a charity. For example, trustees of a charity may only be paid where the constitution contains such a power and it can be considered to be in the best interests of the charity. In practice this is rare. The founder of a social enterprise – an entrepreneur with philanthropic intentions, for example – who nonetheless wishes to be paid cannot be on the board of a charity and must give up ultimate control of the organisation to a volunteer board, which she might well find unacceptable. This restriction does not apply to CICs, which should therefore find favour with the new breed of individuals who style themselves 'social entrepreneurs'. Furthermore, the definition of 'community interest' that applies to CICs is much wider than the 'public interest' test for charity. Indeed, a CIC can be established for any lawful purpose as long as it is carried on for the benefit of the community, and is not a political party or created to support a political party. On the other hand, although CICs will benefit from the credibility that comes with not-for-profit status, they will not receive the same tax benefits as registered charities.

More importantly, CICs are limited companies, and may be set up either as private companies with shareholders, companies limited by guarantee, or as PLCs. CICs will be able to pay their shareholders dividends, so long as they comply with certain 'caps' and restrictions. Despite these, CICs thus have access to an important source of finance (share capital) additional to the sources social enterprises have benefited from over the years, and though CICs themselves do not have many tax benefits, investors in CICs can and will probably continue to be able to benefit from some tax concessions. CICs can also establish and own 'normal' subsidiaries without any of the restrictions on equity that apply to CICs themselves, thus allowing them some facility for setting up and financing ventures that need the benefit of normal risk finance.

Although the regulatory environment for CICs is much lighter than that for charities, CICs are still required to report annually to their own regulator. Included in their annual reports must be comments on how they have involved their stakeholders in their affairs. It is worth noting that, in addition to complying with the CIC regulations, a CIC is also a limited company and therefore subject to the same regulations and statutes as other limited companies. The advent of the CIC marks an interesting and important development in the management and governance of social enterprises.

The governance challenges presented by and facing not-for-profits and social enterprises serve to illustrate that though money and ownership are important influences on the governance agenda, they are not the only ones. What is true for charities is also, to varying degrees, true for other organisations as well.

3 Sources of finance

Alleyn: Who are you?
Fennyman: I'm … um … I'm the money.
Alleyn: Then you may remain. So long as you
remain silent.

Shakespeare in Love, Marc Norman and Tom Stoppard

Money pumps through the heart of any organisation. Even those business organisations led by people who claim to be really interested in other things depend on money as a body depends on blood. And organisations that run out of it suffer the same fate as a body deprived of its blood supply. Otherwise healthy businesses in 2008 and 2009 were being struck down with alarming regularity. Businesses big and small were reporting that their financiers – their suppliers of money – were rewriting agreements, or demanding new terms, or in some instances offering no terms at all. No money: no business. A client of mine, not alone, reported that insurers had refused to extend credit insurance to its suppliers, thus cutting off its ability to purchase on credit the goods which it was then planning to distribute at a margin to its customers. At one remove this is another manifestation of blockages in the arteries supplying cash. Supplier, distributor and end-customer all suffered from what was principally an unwillingness or inability to move cash between businesses up and

is not applicable.

down the supply chain and around the economic system. Making money may or may not be the principal objective of an organisation, but finding it, attracting it, looking after it, protecting it, and applying it properly and efficiently are key governance issues for all types of organisation.

Other people's money

Seeking and receiving investment from an external source – 'other people's money' – is often one of the first stimuli prompting an entrepreneur or owner-manager to think about governance. At its simplest, banks will want to see that the business is well organised and appropriately managed. They will want to see the accounts, and will want to be sure they tell the truth, and that the truth is the sort of story that warrants the business borrowing money. Receiving an injection of equity finance from a business angel or venture capitalist, or giving equity to a new member of the management team, brings further governance complications. Founders themselves need to adjust their mindsets because ownership now has to be shared. From the founder shareholders' perspective, the prospect of giving away equity for finance can be difficult to stomach. But a smaller share of a well-managed larger business can be worth much more than the whole of a less well-managed smaller business. If the price of recruiting decent management, or securing intelligent investment, is sharing equity, then giving it away can be in the interests of everyone, including the giver. A common mistake of founders is to confuse ownership with control. You can afford to share major slugs of equity with others without losing control of the business. Many founders never appreciate the importance of this distinction, nor the flexibility it offers.

Nevertheless, ceding equity will bring change. Giving equity to a financier often leads to the appointment of a non-executive director for the first time – in effect, someone sitting on the board looking after the financier's investment. Giving equity to a new member of management brings its own complications: a new member of the management team who was not there at the beginning will have a different relationship with the business than the founder. Yes, a slice of equity will help bring everyone together, but founders should never forget that a second-generation equity holder will never have the same paternal instincts about the business as founders.

When considering the governance implications of different types of financial stakeholder, it needs to be remembered that different types of financier have different concerns. As already noted, money is not just supplied by shareholders putting their capital at risk, it is also supplied by banks and other lenders. External shareholders invest at risk in return for profit, either in the form of dividends or as surplus returns when the shares are sold. Banks lend against security in return for interest. If the business does well and profits are large, banks do not benefit – at least not directly – but shareholders do. Conversely, of course, if the business does less well and does not turn a profit, then the shareholders might not get anything at all, but the bank will still expect its interest. And if catastrophe strikes, though the shareholder can expect to lose everything, including her capital, the bank at least can redeem its security and receive back some (or in some instances all) of its money. So shareholders and banks are two sources of money, with two different types of interest in the business, both of which need safeguarding. Although they are both providers of money, to a certain extent their interests conflict. Corporate governance mechanisms are thus needed to protect both types of provider of finance from each other.

Shareholders will argue that their need for protection against management is greater than banks'. Banks can and do, as noted above, lend against security. They have the opportunity to scrutinise the assets put up for security before deciding whether a loan applicant is good for the money – hence the cynical observation of many a cash-starved businessman, that banks only want to lend you money when you do not need really it. But banks will argue in return that in most businesses it is they rather than the shareholders who are really at one remove from management. In the vast majority of businesses, management and shareholders are the same people. If governance is designed to protect 'Mr Money' from management, then for many businesses this surely means protecting the interests of the bank from the shareholders.

There is another complication. Shareholders in incorporated companies have the benefit of limited liability. They risk the capital they invest in an opportunity, but that is all they risk. If the business goes bust, that investment is all they will lose. They will not, unless they have acted wrongfully, be pursued by the company's creditors for outstanding debts. If their liability was unlimited they might have at risk their houses and their other personal assets, as is indeed the case for the owners of unincorporated entities, such as partners in traditional partnerships. This gives shareholders in limited companies some advantages over the owners of unincorporated entities: their upside is not capped, but their downside is. This puts them at some advantage compared with other individuals involved in the same business – a potential supplier, or a potential employee thinking of giving up a well-paid, secure job elsewhere to join the company. Yes, a shareholder in a business that is in difficulty might well have to think about putting up some money to pay the wage bill to keep the company going, but this is a choice, not an absolute liability. And closer shareholders might be expected to know more about what is going on at a company than more distant shareholders, and might therefore be able to make a more informed choice.

The point is perhaps better appreciated when we consider those individuals who are responsible for unincorporated organisations and who are therefore exposed to the perils of unlimited liability without even knowing it. Many social enterprises, including many charities, continue to be unincorporated organisations. Yes, such organisations do enjoy some freedoms that incorporated organisations are not allowed, but an unincorporated charity, for example, as a *charity* is still subject to the prescriptions of the Charity Commission. Because they are unincorporated such organisations do not provide any limitation to liability for their principal officers or governors – an important weakness that many people involved in such organisations in my experience are just not aware of, nor of the potential implications this might have for their personal and financial security. To benefit from the protection of limited liability a charity will have to register as a company (usually a company limited by guarantee) as well as a charity. In the future the introduction of a new vehicle currently called a Charitable Incorporated Organisation (CIO) might change this, and enable an organisation to set itself up as a charity and an incorporated entity in one step, but this is still, at the time of writing, a matter under consultation.

Limited liability has done much for economic development in the world. Some would argue that it has been the single most important contributor to the economic success of the West. But because limited liability puts shareholders in a position of advantage, some would argue that we need governance mechanisms to protect other stakeholders from the shareholders, not the other way round. Indeed, it is the advantages bestowed on shareholders by limited liability that helps explain why limited companies are required to publish accounts when traditional unlimited partnerships do not.

Who really needs looking after?

Governance in great part exists to govern the relationships between financial stakeholders and managers, and between other stakeholders and financial stakeholders. But as financial systems and structures have got more complicated, globalised and real-time, it has become increasingly difficult to separate out the interests of bank, shareholder and manager, along with the tensions and conflicts, potential and real, between them. It is thus much harder to work out who needs protecting from whom and because of what.

Take the example of the fashion towards the end of the last boom for the share buy-back. Led by managers, and egged on by shareholders, both long-term and activist, companies bought back their own shares, often using significant increases of debt to finance the restructuring. Such acquisitions reduced the number of shares in issue, and increased therefore their price – though at a time when share prices seemed to be increasing anyway it is a moot point as to the extent to which the buy-backs made any difference. One journalist described the share buy-back as 'the must have fashion accessory for any up-and-coming company'.[19] At the time nobody seemed to object much: shareholders received either cash or an increased share price; bankers received a significant new source of earnings from the newly issued debt; managers received bigger bonuses, no doubt because they were incentivised at least in part to deliver higher earnings per share, which a reduction of shares in issue could only facilitate. City advisers and brokers no doubt cheered them all on their way, not unconscious of the fees they were earning from such transactions. Indeed, on 16 November 2007, with the FTSE-100 standing at almost 6,300, a total of 77 companies announced that they had been into the market to purchase their own equity,[20] including Alliance & Leicester, which in 2006 spent a total of £150 million acquiring its own shares as they soared to more than £12 each. Yet within eight months the board of the now cash-strapped Alliance & Leicester accepted an all-share offer from Banco Santander that put a value of just 317p a share on the company. Alliance & Leicester were not alone. HBOS bought 250,000 of its own shares in November 2007 at a price of 783½p, but a year later HBOS shares were trading for about a tenth of that price. Property companies and others indulged in the same folly, buying their own shares at high prices and saddling their businesses with debt.

With the benefit of hindsight it is easy to see that the vogue for the share buy-back was at best short-sighted and misguided. The circumstances that led to this particular failure suggest also an over-reliance on the personal interests of several individual groups of stakeholder, and a failure to put the long-term interests of the company first. In other words, this is a failure of governance, and good governance practice is all about structures and practices that prevent such self-interest and short-termism getting in the way of sound strategy and effective management.

It is evident from this example that governance is subject to fashion as the economy rises and falls. When times are good, cash on the balance sheet is an evil: businesses are encouraged to have as little of it as possible. A business with too much cash on its balance sheet is not making proper use of its resources, indicating an inability to identify and exploit opportunities that are out there, which in turn reflects on the competence of management. When times are good businesses are therefore urged to make their balance sheets 'efficient'. Getting rid of cash from the balance sheet is seen to be in the interests of shareholders. However, when times are bad, prudent organisations ensure their businesses are sufficiently 'liquid'. Balance sheet *efficiency* is replaced by balance sheet *viability* as the principal concern. In autumn 2008 nervous auditors started asking questions about even established organisations' abilities to roll over what just the year before would have been considered routine loans before signing off on 'going concern'.

But the role of money in governance is not just a function of economic cycles. When share prices went into free fall in 2008, shareholders found it only too easy to identify people to blame for the decline in value of their investments in many major companies. Institutional investors pointed fingers at non-executives and regulators, the bastions of most governance regimes. But who were the shareholders asking the corporate governance regimen to protect them from? They were asking for protection from themselves. To a certain extent corporate governance does indeed have this function as well – not protecting one party from another, but safeguarding the interests of all.

When economic circumstances worsen it is almost inevitable that those with financial stakes in organisations take governance more seriously. For example, the financially weak but innocent, who managed to survive, even to profit, when times were good, find themselves exposed, and fall like ninepins when times are bad. Again they look for someone, or something, to blame. Furthermore, as the financial tide recedes further from the shore, all sorts of unpleasant flotsam and jetsam are left on the beach, including the scoundrels and conmen of all sorts who preyed on the greed and ambitions of those keen to do better than they deserved in the bull market. Bernard Madoff's strategies have cost his investors perhaps $50 billion. We see his like in every recession. J.K. Galbraith observed of the 1929 crash and the ensuring depression:

> To the economist embezzlement is the most interesting
> of crimes. Alone among the various forms of larceny it

has a time parameter. Weeks, months or years may elapse between the commission of the crime and its discovery. (This is a period, incidentally, when the embezzler has his gain and the man who has been embezzled, oddly enough, feels no loss. There is a net increase in psychic wealth.) At any given time there exists an inventory of undiscovered embezzlement in – or more precisely not in – the country's business and banks. This inventory – it should perhaps be called the bezzle – amounts at any moment to many millions of dollars. It also varies in size with the business cycle. In good times people are relaxed, trusting, and money is plentiful. But even though money is plentiful, there are always many people who need more. Under these circumstances the rate of embezzlement grows, the rate of discovery falls off, and the bezzle increases rapidly. In depression all this is reversed. Money is watched with a narrow, suspicious eye. The man who handles it is assumed to be dishonest until he proves himself otherwise. Audits are penetrating and meticulous. Commercial morality is enormously improved. The bezzle shrinks.[21]

As the recession that started in 2008 matures and the world faces up to the prospect of paying down the biggest store of 'psychic wealth' ever brewed in a financial alchemist's laboratory, expect the attitudes of those worried about the safety of their own money to sharpen. Expect them also to call with increasing stridency for corporate governance mechanisms to protect them. But expect everyone – investors, regulators and alchemists – to relax again when the good times come back.

4 | People

'Many people genuinely do not want to be saints, and it is probable that some who achieve or aspire to sainthood have never felt much temptation to be human beings.'

George Orwell[22]

For many people governance is all about rules. But good governance is at least as much about roles and the people who fill them. Robert Simons of Harvard Business School makes a case for management rather than capital being the critical resource in business, as a consequence of which he argues that businesses should measure 'return on management' rather than 'return on equity' or 'return on capital employed'.[23] In this chapter we will explore the commonest roles around the boardroom or the senior management table in the context of governance. We will discuss people in all sorts of roles in all sorts of organisations, including those organisations that straddle the barriers between conventional stereotypes.

The top job – managing directors, chairmen and entrepreneurs

Andrea: Unhappy the land that needs heroes ...
Galileo: No, unhappy the land where heroes are needed.

The Life of Galileo, Bertolt Brecht

In the UK we often call the 'top job' the 'managing director'. But nowadays most large businesses in the UK will have a chairman as well, and the role of chairman is different from the role of MD. The chairman will chair the board and in a big business will act more often than not in a non-executive capacity. The managing director is the executive head of the business – a different role demanding a different sort of individual.

In the US, businesses big and small tend not to have chairmen, but rather 'presidents'. The title of 'president' is one Americanism that has found little favour in the UK, just as the title 'king' has never gone down that well in the US. But by contrast, the title 'chief executive officer' is an Americanism that has stuck and is now commonly used in the UK as an alternative to the title 'managing director'. Undoubtedly the American title is meant to have grander connotations than the older title of managing director, and to some ears the notion of 'execution' does sound somewhat more dynamic than 'direction'.

In the US, and increasingly in the UK, businesses will boast both a chief executive and a chief operating officer (COO), with the latter mainly responsible for implementing the former's strategy. Some will argue that the appointment of a COO is a way of segmenting and sharing the CEO's role – a recognition that the role is too big for one person. In the US, even more than in the UK, the big-business CEO will be a 'lone ranger', reporting to the board rather than part of it, with significant personal authority. As businesses have become more sophisticated it seems logical at least to split the role. On the other hand, research by Donald Hambrick of Smeal College of Business at Penn State University suggests that organisations with COOs have inferior performance compared with those without.[24] A CEO in need of a COO is in some cases a CEO who cannot cope – and the reason for that might be related to the CEO's competence rather than capacity. More charitably it should be noted that in the US it is commonplace to combine the roles of CEO and chairman. When it comes to the top job, rather than separate out the role of chairman it is more common to separate out the role of COO.

In the UK, unlike the US, good governance practice for listed businesses recommends that the roles of chairman and chief executive/managing director are separated. The Combined Code sets this out clearly enough as a 'main principle':

> There should be a clear division of responsibilities at the head of the company between the running of the board and the executive responsibility for the running of the company's business. No one individual should have unfettered powers of decision.[25]

Although the Combined Code invites a 'comply or explain' approach to its own provisions, businesses that do not separate out the roles of chairman and chief executive often have a hard time with activist shareholders, not to mention the press. Segregating duties is a key principle of any control system, as junior accountants learn in their first year of studies. An individual in the accounts department who has too much involvement in too many processes is in a position to be able to cook the books. The same is true in the boardroom, which is why in the UK at least it is considered important to separate the two top roles. On the other hand, shackling the key decision taker might be argued to be not in the interests of efficient decision taking. As Napoleon observed, it is better to have one bad general than two good ones, and he would undoubtedly have favoured the strong direction that a single point of leadership brings to a company. (Champions of splitting the role of chairman and chief executive will be quick to point out what happened to Napoleon.)

When the two roles are merged, the individual concerned often gets the title of 'executive chairman'. Semantically an 'executive chairman' is only a chairman who also happens to have an executive role. However, if the chairman does have an executive role it will almost inevitably be the most important executive role in the business. Even if a separate chief executive is identified, an executive chairman is likely to be the one calling the shots. In March 2008, off the back of failing to find a new CEO, Marks & Spencer announced that their CEO, while remaining chief executive, was also to take on the role of chairman. Institutional investors protested noisily in the press. George Dallas, Director of Corporate Governance at F&C Asset Management, said: 'It is not something we see as a progressive step in the company's governance.'[26] Others were not so delicate. Richard Buxton, head of UK Equities at Schroders, which at the time held about 2 per cent of M&S, said: 'For such a household name to do this sets an appalling precedent. They should reverse the decision and appoint an independent chairman. Rose is sufficiently arrogant to say that if you do not want me to take this role, I will leave. I would actually face up to that. The company is bigger than any individual.'[27]

The Combined Code is principally aimed at large listed businesses, and, by implication, some of the principles need not apply to other types of business – for example large private businesses or smaller listed businesses. In the opening chapter of this book I noted that when Alliance Boots was

taken private by private equity in 2007 its biggest shareholder, Stefano Pessina, took the role of executive chairman,
thus merging the two top roles, just as in Marks & Spencer.
Now the privately owned Alliance Boots no longer needed
to 'comply or explain' its adherence to the provisions of
the Combined Code, compliance ceased to matter, but this
did not stop Pessina from getting a hammering in the press.
One interpretation of Pessina's change of role is that Alliance
Boots was previously complying with the Combined Code,
not because it believed the guidance to separate the roles of
CEO and chairman was useful or significant, but for the sake
of complying with the rule. An alternative interpretation is
that Alliance Boots believed the guidance made sense for
listed companies, but not for private businesses. Though still
responsible for the same large business, Pessina became in
effect an owner-manager.

Do the duties and responsibilities of the top role really
change as a business gets bigger or as it changes form? Titles
change. The title of chief executive does not sit easily with
many younger, growing businesses, while 'managing director' has had a longer life in business than 'chief executive',
and is both broader and more precise at the same time. There
are some big businesses that sport chief executives, chief
operating officers *and* managing directors, presuming a fine
distinction between them. But many leaders of younger businesses content themselves with just a managing director. It
carries within it both the role of chief executive and chief
operating officer, executor and operator, strategist and tac-
tician. The title of managing director perhaps suggests connotations associated with governance and stewardship, as
well as decision taking and management. A small business
may have a managing director and a big business may have
an executive chairman: in both cases, regardless of size, form
and shareholding, the key decisions are in the control of a

very powerful individual. And it is only a small series of steps in the argument from this line of thinking to a conclusion that Pessina at Alliance Boots and Rose at Marks & Spencer are really attempting to run their businesses as small, owner-managed businesses, and are failing to pay due respect to the changes that size brings. Power concentrated in the hands of one individual, in the UK at least, is more acceptable in a small business than in a big one, regardless of titles.

David Ross's problems at the end of 2008 with Carphone Warehouse were possibly of a similar kind. Ross resigned from the board of Carphone Warehouse, a listed company, after admitting offering his shares in the company as security for personal loans – a practice in breach of London Stock Exchange regulations, at least if not disclosed. Ross had also offered as security his shares in Big Yellow Group and National Express without disclosure. Although a director of listed businesses and a chartered accountant, Ross, it was claimed by his supporters, had just made an honest mistake. Indeed the FSA subsequently noted that the law governing this area – the EU Market Abuse Directive – was unclear, and took no further action against him. Luke Johnson, restaurant entrepreneur and Chairman of Channel 4, said:

> Britain needs bold entrepreneurs more than ever if we are to create new jobs and maintain our standard of living. We need to encourage people to take risks – not bury them when they make a slip-up like this. No wonder so much talent wants nothing to do with public companies.[28]

But it might be argued that at heart Ross's actions demonstrated his reluctance to adjust to the demands and responsibilities of being the director of a listed company. Stelios Haji-Ioannou's evolving relationship with EasyJet is interesting in this regard. 'Starting a company requires a very different skill-set from those needed to chair a major plc, and I consider my strengths are in the former,' Stelios noted, when resigning as chairman of EasyJet in April 2002. 'The history of the City is littered with entrepreneurs who held on to their creations for too long, failing to recognise the changing needs of the company.'[29] I wonder whether Stelios remembered these words when, in a very public row with management in November 2008, he argued that the company's growth strategy needed reining back, and a dividend needed paying by 2011. If he did not get his way, Stelios threatened to exercise a right reserved to him: as long as he held more than 25 per cent of the shares, he would have the right to appoint two non-executive directors. So long as he held more than 10 per cent, he also retained the right to make himself chairman. The agreement could not be changed 'unless approved by a resolution of the board, at which an independent non-executive is in the majority'.

The source of Stelios's unusual power lay in a 'Relationship Agreement' drafted at the time of EasyJet's float. To be fair, the document stated that the company should have its own management, and that it should 'make decisions for the benefit of shareholders as a whole and independently of the controlling shareholders at all times'. Stelios noted: 'I am merely applying my rights under the articles of incorporation of the company to protect my investment.'[30] The row continued to simmer through 2009, and in April 2009 EasyJet chairman Sir Colin Chandler announced he was resigning early. The newspapers reported him as being 'Fed up with the situation of running a board, which is tough. You have got a recession, there are some strong characters on the board and public companies these days are very tough to run.' Stelios for his part was reported as describing the situation as a 'debate, not a dispute'.[31] By July 2009, with the airline industry in crisis, Stelios was seen to have won the argument; EasyJet were scaling back on their plans. Some even described it as a triumph of the entrepreneur over the money men.

The case of the 'Phoenix Four' also throws interesting light on the relationship between the board and entrepreneurship and how things change when businesses get bigger – and then smaller again. The car industry in the UK was founded by a generation of enterprising engineers and entrepreneurs running independent firms. By the time British Leyland dominated the industrial landscape as a nationalised conglomerate the founders' names were little more than vestigial badges on second-rate models that competed inefficiently with each other. The government sold the group to BAE who then sold it on to BMW. BMW sold the assets of the Rover Group to the Phoenix Consortium in 2000. Initially hailed as heroes for developing a plan that promised to save jobs and maintain mainstream car manufacturing under UK ownership, the Phoenix Four were subsequently vilified when the business was put into administration – vilified not so much for failing, but for the £42 million in pay and pensions they paid to themselves while they were at the helm. Here again, apparently, was an example of a board who had failed to balance appropriately the competing interests of different groups of stakeholders; who behaved as if their own interests should come first; who acted in many ways as if they were running an owner-managed business. Of course, the fact that they *were* running an owner-managed business, albeit one they only paid £10 for, should not be used as an excuse for arguing that the interests of the employees and customers, not to mention taxpayers who pumped a lot of money into the enterprise, were less important than their own. Like the MPs benefiting from the expenses system at Westminster, the Phoenix Four claimed they had 'done nothing wrong'.

Several of these stories suggest some difficulty reconciling the roles of director and entrepreneur. They also suggest a tendency in the minds of entrepreneurs to blur the distinction between the role of chief executive and chairman. But, as noted already, the role of chairman is different from the role of managing director or chief executive. The role of chief executive we have already discussed, and we have also referred to the temptation to merge the role of chairman and chief executive – the reality, indeed, in the US. What about the role of chairman pure and simple?

The role of chairman is to chair the board, which is quite different from leading the company. The chairman's authority reaches little further than the boardroom. But this is not to diminish the role at all. As the chairman of the board rather than the company the chairman is responsible for the effectiveness of the board as the senior decision-taking forum. It is the chairman and not the chief executive who leads the board. Board leadership involves chairing board meetings, of course, and includes facilitating the involvement of non-executive directors. Board leadership also involves ensuring that communication channels with shareholders, active and passive, and other stakeholders are open and effective. The chairman is responsible for the agenda of the board. In addition, board leadership involves holding the chief executive to account. As noted above, holding the executive team to account is difficult if the chairman is also an executive. Effective chairmanship is about the processes of management rather than management itself. Ultimately, therefore, effective chairmanship is at the heart of good governance.

Changing nature of the top role

Founding entrepreneurs have often expressed disquiet at the changes brought to their companies by growth and success – in particular the governance pressures brought by flotation. 'Did flotation work?' asked Anita Roddick when promoting her book *Business as Unusual* in 2001. 'Well, it gave us money to build manufacturing plants ... Does it work now? I do not think so. [The Body Shop has] lost its soul since floating on the stock market ... it has no place as a cog in the international finance system ... . [The Body Shop] is now really a dysfunctional coffin.' Anita Roddick described attempting to take her business private again on at least two occasions, so that she could do business away from the glare of investor scrutiny. Sir Richard Branson cheerfully floated Virgin on the stock market, but bought it back again in 1998, stating: 'Being an entrepreneur and the chairman of a public company just don't mix.'

Perhaps more interesting is Pret A Manger founder Julian Metcalfe. 'You've got to be a bit of a gambler' Metcalfe told an audience in 1996, still full of entrepreneurial enthusiasm. 'My partner's way of assessing risk is to work out that if we can afford to lose money it will not be a problem. Mine is to do it anyway, because if you feel passionately about something it's probably going to work.'[32] But in 2003, after having stood back and recruited a CEO (who then turned himself into chairman and chief executive), and then having fired the same chairman/CEO when business turned bad, Metcalfe noted: 'I am quite a cautious person deep down. Pret started in 1986 and it took five years before we developed our second shop. It developed in America far too quickly ...' Maybe Metcalfe's change of attitude reflects the conservatism that the passing years bring to most of us; maybe it reflects the changing nature of the top job.

The problem of the changing nature of the top role also presents itself when new businesses succeed and grow dramatically, and their founders hang on to the reins. How does the role change? To what extent does the governance agenda change? In an interesting article,[33] John Hamm argues that founders flounder when they try to manage the bigger organisation. Hamm claims to have identified four tendencies that work for the leaders of smaller companies but that become Achilles' heels when they try to manage a larger organisation: loyalty to comrades; task orientation; single-mindedness; and working in isolation. All of these are strengths. But loyalty, if blind, can turn into a liability; task orientation can develop into an excessive attention to detail and an inability to delegate; single-mindedness can ossify into tunnel vision; and the ability to work alone can be 'disastrous for a leader whose burgeoning organisation must rely on the kindness of customers, investors, analysts, reporters and other strangers'.

Hamm is acute in his analysis – though he is a little unkind in his fourth 'strength'. If there is only room in a business for one managing director, and the managing director needs to be different from what has gone before, it stands to reason that the role of managing director is pretty lonely. Many managing directors acknowledge the paradox. They spend their days talking to colleagues and customers, yet they are alone. Getting truly close to other individuals in the business is difficult when you are the boss. Getting your colleagues just to tell you the truth when you're the boss is difficult enough. Which begs questions about the role of the CEO's colleagues on the board of a company, and how they are recruited.

One of the key transitions in the development of an owner-managed business, and a defining moment in the development of a governance agenda in the smallest of businesses, is the moment when founders look to someone other than themselves to carry the senior management mantle – a young business's first managing director. In most cases the trigger is recognising that the business has grown too big and complicated for the skills of the founder. But founders often misunderstand the nature of the change the business is going through and consequently misunderstand the nature of the role they are recruiting for. Several business founders I have advised on recruitment, for example, have said to me: 'What this business really needs is someone else just like me.' But if individuals like the founder exist around the world the last thing they are likely to want to do is go and work for someone else, least of all for someone like themselves – and someone like the founder. Entrepreneurs set out with a new business, determined to do a new thing their own way. Working to someone else's agenda is very far from their minds. An owner-manager keen to keep involved is thus most likely to recruit someone to look after the internal operations of the growing business – more an operating officer, therefore. But an effective managing director will only be effective if he can at least strongly influence external strategy and thus the context within which internal development of the business is to take place.

Recruiting in your own image is not just a problem for owner-managers looking for their first managing director. The problem will re-present itself each time an appointment is made – and for as long as the founder continues to be actively involved in the business. Another common instance when founders instinctively recruit in their own image is in family businesses. Family business founders often look along the line of their offspring, hoping to see the one most able to step into the old man's shoes – and depression sets in when none of the children are quite cut of the same cloth as the business founder. But again, looking for a younger version of yourself in a family business is unlikely to lead to the best appointment. The business will have changed fundamentally since its genesis. Running a business that has already been founded, has passed through the difficult early stages and has reached sustainability is a different prospect from the act of founding and taking a business through those early stages. It requires more discipline and more control; more analysis and less gut feel; more focus on process and less on output; more focus on bottom line and less on top line; more focus on skills, capability and qualifications and less on instinct. It requires someone who can convert personal aspirations into corporate vision and commercial plans. Of course, these are shifts of emphasis and not either/ors, but nevertheless they are indicative of a significant change in the demands made of business leadership as the business develops.

No business founder – even in a family business – should look for a younger version of himself when looking for a successor. He should look for what the business needs now and in the immediate future, not what it needed 25 years ago. A business founder should look for difference and challenge in a new managing director – someone who complements rather than compliments him. And when the time comes to recruit again, the shareholders should look for difference and challenge again, though this time bearing in mind that the needs of the business will have moved on as well.

Directors – executive and non-executive

In many companies the key decision takers are the directors themselves. In others, the directors are the first check on the key decision takers, who are variously called management, or the executives. In the UK the executives tend to be directors anyway, and are joined in their deliberations around the table by non-executive directors – individuals without direct executive responsibility but with joint responsibility for the company. In the US, executive responsibility tends to be more focused on the single figure of the CEO, with the directors tending to be mostly independent and at one superior remove. In Germany executive directors tend to sit on a junior, operational board that reports to a senior supervisory board of non-executives. In charities the directors, often called trustees, are usually non-executive, and frequently are unpaid. In big charities, the trustees are responsible for an organisation that is often run by a group of paid executive managers. In smaller charities the trustees exercise the responsibilities of management themselves. In all these cases the involvement of directors in important decision taking is a problematic issue, for executives, directors (executive or otherwise) and other stakeholders trying to get a handle on where the organisation is heading and why.

Unsurprisingly, therefore, directors are the occasion and the object of much corporate governance. Regardless of the structure of the board, they are the people responsible for ensuring their companies are up to scratch. For many people, directors are also the villains that corporate governance was invented to sort out. As the credit crunch deepened in 2008, Lord Myners, subsequently appointed Financial Services Secretary to the Treasury from October 2008, wrote in the *Financial Times*: 'The typical bank board resembles a retirement home for the great and the good: there are retired titans of industry, ousted politicians and the occasional member of the voluntary sector. If such a selection ... was ever good enough, it is not now.'[34]

It is important to distinguish those directors who are recognised as directors of limited companies under company law, and those who just carry the title on their business cards. The former will be registered as such at Companies House, and their names will be on the financial statements. The latter will have been given the title because it carries with it status inside the business or with clients. Many of the most senior staff members in professional service firms carry the title 'director', but in company law terms they are not. Some of them, indeed, do not even work for limited companies but rather for partnerships, in which case senior staff who are not partners are often called directors to distinguish them from senior managers.

Individuals who call themselves 'directors', but are not directors of a limited company they work for in the legal sense, need to be careful not to be confused with the real thing. Conversely, in extremis, a court might well look for individuals who have not signed the forms, but have been the ones really responsible for taking the decisions and who are deemed to be directors regardless. Advisers, bank managers and others make sure their terms of engagement clearly indicate they are not directors, nor 'shadow directors' (individuals who seem to be acting as if they are directors).

The directors are charged with supervising the governance and management of the company. This is worthy of comment. The directors are acting in the interests of the company, not the shareholders. This is a subtle distinction that is much misunderstood. In the UK, however, the matter is now expressly referred to in the Companies Act 2006, which states that a director has a 'duty to promote the success of the company'.

The directors' duty to the company becomes particularly important when the shareholders cannot agree with each other, or, indeed, when a director is appointed in effect by one set of shareholders. Regardless of the interests that have seen an individual acquire a seat on the board, once on it their duty is to act in the interests of the company as a whole, not any one constituency in particular. Indeed, the Companies Act 2006 now imposes a specific duty on directors to 'exercise independent judgement' (Section 173). Similarly, the interests of the company take priority over the personal interests of any directors, and also over the interests of their particular fiefdoms in the company. The fact that a sales director might direct the sales department does not mean she is not ultimately responsible, along with the other directors, for the direction of the company as a whole. When acting as a director, at least, the interests of the company must be put first.

It is different for shareholders, for whom it is much more a case of everyone for themselves. Shareholders are allowed to act in their own interests rather than in the notional interest of the company of which they have chosen to be members. The shareholders do not ordinarily *as shareholders* have any role running the business day to day, but pass this responsibility to the directors, whom they, the shareholders, appoint. What then of the director who owns shares? As a shareholder, a shareholding director can be expected to vote in his own interests and not those of the company. However, if he is a majority shareholder he has to be careful not to act unfairly against minority shareholders, in which case the latter might object that the relevant resolutions are not in the interests of the company as a whole. A shareholder who is a director needs to remember to act as a director in the boardroom. A key occasion when the conflict might raise its head is when one or more of the directors seek to effect a management buyout. Of course, the decision to recommend approval of the MBO should be taken only by those board members not participating in the deal. However, it should be always remembered that it is *all* directors who have a responsibility for ensuring any transaction is in the best interests of the shareholders – including those fronting the deal itself. A director who is also a shareholder needs therefore to remember which hat he is wearing. He also needs to remember when he is wearing it – in a shareholders' meeting or a board meeting of the directors.

All directors have to be careful to distinguish between acts they commit on behalf of the company and acts they commit in a personal capacity. As a director, an individual represents his company when he negotiates with others on his company's behalf. When signing documents, the director should make sure he discloses that he signs as a director of a company whose full name is given, otherwise he might be deemed to be signing as himself, and therefore be personally liable for the contracts. Again, the Companies Act 2006 now imposes an express duty (set out in Section 175) on directors to avoid conflicts of interest. Indeed, from October 2008, directors must specifically be authorised by their board if they place themselves in a position where they may face a conflict of interest. Even more starkly, the Companies Act 2006 also now introduces a duty 'not to accept benefits from third parties' (Section 176). This is an evolving area of law and we await developments with interest. Directors who step into some of the inevitable grey areas do so at their peril. Particular attention should be paid if the business is courting insolvency, when the interests of other stakeholders including employees and creditors become even more important – more important than the interests of shareholders.

Problems caused by conflicts between the owner side and the manager side of the brain of owner-managers have practical implications for the health of the business and the equanimity of owner-managers, and they also have legalistic implications. A director who is also a shareholder, as well as father of two of the company's senior managers, and married to the finance director, is in a far weaker position than, say, a venture capitalist when it comes to a heated discussion about issues of importance. The venture capitalist is motivated only by money. Suffering from none of the tensions facing the owner-manager-father-husband-employer, the financier is in a stronger negotiating position when the going gets tough.

The Companies Act 2006, as noted, gives express attention for the first time to the duties of directors and how they should go about discharging their duties. In Section 172(1) the Act lists specific matters that (among others) a director should consider when determining whether or not she is promoting the success of the company for 'the benefit of its members as a whole'. The list includes the following:

(a) the likely consequences of any decision in the long term,

(b) the interests of the company's employees,

(c) the need to foster the company's business relationships with suppliers, customers and others,

(d) the impact of the company's operations on the community and the environment,

(e) the desirability of the company maintaining a reputation for high standards of business conduct, and

(f) The need to act fairly as between members of the company.

There is now little doubt in UK law at least that the duties of a director are broad, and encompass responsibilities far beyond looking after the shareholders; and certainly extend beyond feathering their own nests. The list also has implications for the competence of directors and their access to information.

Non-executive directors in particular

A venture capitalist, or someone else with a significant financial interest, might well demand a seat on the board as a condition of investing. Such an appointment is usually as a non-executive, but if you are wondering exactly what a non-executive director is, do not expect to get much help from the law. Apparently it is one of the most important functions within any company, but although statute has a lot to say about directors it has little to say about the distinction between the executive and non-executive kinds. The Companies Act 2006 continues this tradition by not making any meaningful distinction. Such differences as there are arise from case law and current practice, and also from codes and frameworks, which have certainly had a lot to say about the particular role of the non-executive. But from a legal point of view, executive directors and non-executive directors have similar responsibilities and are exposed to similar risks.

The most important point to stress, therefore, is that as far as the law is concerned there is not much difference at all between a non-executive director and an executive director. Both are responsible for the company as a whole. Nonetheless, for many, the non-executive director is the most important element in any governance framework. If anyone is expected to have responsibility for looking after the interests of shareholders and safeguarding them from aberrant directors (executive, of course), it is the non-executive. Indeed even in a private business in which the majority owners are the directors, a non-executive who is representing the interests of a financial investor does indeed have a role safeguarding the interests of investors who might not otherwise have an influence on the direction of the business.

In one sense, the role of director is itself a non-executive role. When acting as directors even executives need to take themselves away from their day-to-day executive responsibilities (and the prejudices that go with them) and consider the interests of the company as a whole. This is what non-executives do all the time; but it is what executives do only when acting as and taking decisions as directors.

So what then is the difference between a non-executive and an executive? Perhaps the best way of encapsulating this is to imagine a sliding scale between two sets of opposites:

Executive	Non-executive
Hands-on	Hands-off
Not independent	Independent
Full-time	Part-time
Employed	Self-employed
Strategist	Policeman
Internal knowledge	External knowledge

It is too easy at times to see definitions in terms of black and white, which is perhaps why statute has fought shy of coming up with a definition of a non-executive director. Assuming you are happy dealing with tendencies, it is fair to observe that non-executive directors tend not to be involved with day-to-day management. In the past 'hands-off' has led to the title 'non-executive director' often signifying a big name who adorns a company letterhead, turns up for the sherry after the meeting and treats the meeting itself as a rest before the sherry. In the current business world 'hands-off' for the non-executive suggests someone who is not encumbered with *specific* management responsibility. There will be no reporting lines into a non-executive – dotted or otherwise. However, 'hands-off' cannot be taken too far: non-executives have never been formally absolved from management responsibility. They are and always were part of the board ultimately responsible for the day-to-day management of the business. The actual mechanics of day-to-day management may well be an executive responsibility, but ultimate responsibility for the management is shared with the non-executives. In a smaller business, active involvement of the non-executive in day-to-day management is more likely than in a big business – indeed, many small businesses would find it difficult to countenance recruiting a non-executive who was not prepared to get dirt under his fingernails. 'Hands-off' in the small business thus often means little more than 'without portfolio', or not specifically responsible for any one part of the business more than another, but not afraid of interfering where necessary.

'Independent' is often used as a more accurate description of non-executives – or perhaps to describe the key quality that many would like their non-executives to possess. Non-executives are particularly associated with independence when corporate governance is being discussed in big business. Unsurprisingly, for some, being seen to be independent in this context is perhaps even more important than actually being independent. But in reality the label 'independent' again describes a tendency. The fact that the Combined Code requires 'at least half the board, excluding the chairman' of all but small companies to be independent as well as non-executive suggests how little the two terms have to do with each other in reality. All independent directors are non-executives, because to take executive responsibility for a part or all of the business will inevitably prejudice that individual's ability to step back and review the performance of that business objectively. Not all non-executives are independent. Some entrepreneurial businesses, for example, as has already been observed, have non-executives imposed on them by venture capitalists. Such directors are 'independent' of the company, but they are nevertheless not truly independent. Indeed, their role is primarily to safeguard the interests of the venture capitalist, which often clash with those of the company, let alone, potentially, the interests of the other shareholders. As already noted, such directors need to be mindful that, notwithstanding their route to the boardroom table, their duty is to the company as a whole, not to any one shareholder in particular.

Independence itself is a quality that is difficult to pin down, and surprisingly difficult to define. Take the board of Apple in 2002, for example. This board, although directing a huge business, had characteristics that many smaller businesses will find all too familiar. It had only five members in addition to the CEO. Of these, one, though nominally independent under US guidelines, and the chair of the company's audit committee, formerly worked at Apple, and sold his own software business to Apple.[35] Is an individual such as this really independent? The following characteristics are perhaps indicative of a state of independence:

- The individual has not been employed by the company recently, and thus is not predisposed either for or against some parts of the business.

- The individual is not a retained professional adviser, and thus not influenced either by his fee or by judgements taken by another organisation in which he has an interest.

- The individual is not a supplier or customer of the company, and thus likely to influence the company towards or away from one contract or another.

- The individual does not have a family connection with someone in the business.

- The individual does not hold cross directorships or have significant links with other directors by way of involvement with other companies.

- The individual's directorship is for a fixed term, and the individual is therefore less likely to be motivated by self-preservation when taking decisions.

- The individual does not depend so heavily on her remuneration from the company as to make resignation difficult.

The ability – and willingness – to resign is the ultimate test of independence. Unsurprisingly, recommendations and guidelines that have emanated from the various corporate governance reviews in recent years almost always include the obligatory resignation of the non-executives after a specified period of years. An interesting test of this characteristic is again the non-executive who makes a seat on the board a condition of his investment. Such an individual is hardly likely to agree to his own compulsory resignation. But then neither is he really to be thought of as independent. A non-executive with share options might also be argued to have compromised his independence – and corporate governance guidelines tend to frown on such arrangements too. The Combined Code notes: 'Remuneration for non-executive directors should not include share options.' Then, in a splendid flourish of self-contradiction, the same code observes:

> If, exceptionally, options are granted, shareholder
> approval should be sought in advance and any shares
> acquired by exercise of the options should be held until
> at least one year after the non-executive director leaves
> the board. Holding of share options could be relevant
> to the determination of a non-executive director's
> independence.[36]

Independence is an important quality for non-executives in smaller, private businesses as well, though in different ways and with different consequences than for non-executives in big businesses. For a non-executive to support the management team of the smaller business, he has to have a greater degree of independence from it than the executives – an ability to step back and see the wood from the trees, and a more detached commitment to the business than that expected of executives who on occasion can get a little overexcited. What matters in the smaller business is independence of mind rather than independence defined in terms of relationships and financial interests. Independence in this sense is a personal attribute, and it is more valuable to the small company than independence in the listed company sense. Indeed, independence in the latter sense is often almost an irrelevance in the private business that is 100 per cent owned by one or two shareholders. Independence of mind, on the other hand, is priceless.

Almost all non-executive positions are part-time. But here again the 'tendency' rule still applies. Certainly, at times of crisis or times when the non-executives are under particular pressure, the role may well seem full-time. But the fact that the 2009 Walker Report on governance in UK banks recommends a minimum time commitment of 30 to 36 days suggests that part-time is the expectation even in big business. At the beginning of an appointment it is likely to be more – there are people to meet and documents to read. Once established, the work will still involve much more than merely attending board meetings, but still much less than a full-time commitment. The Association of Chartered Certified Accountants' study on the role of non-executives reported that the average amount of time non-executives spend working with 'Small and Medium-Sized Enterprises' is only 18 days a year.

Turning to the next item on our list of opposites, whether or not the role of non-executive is a form of employment is one that is complicated by tax law, which, as so often, has the effect of clouding the issue rather than clarifying it. Tax law has increasingly tended to see employment relationships where there aren't any. But, as a matter of fact, even if not as a matter of tax law, the non-executive role tends to be that of an outsider looking in rather than that of an inside employee. Indeed, whereas many if not most executives will have service contracts as employees to back up their appointments as directors, the majority of non-executives will not, relying on letters of appointment only.

When discussing what a non-executive is in terms of 'tendencies', perhaps the most important trade-off is between 'strategist' and 'policeman' – the role of setting and implementing corporate strategy, and the role of acting as watchdog and whistle-blower for the outside world, ensuring adherence to good practice, respect for the interests of other stakeholders, adherence to the processes of boardroom discipline and so on. If the role of strategist is usually associated with that of the executive, the role of policeman is associated with that of the non-executive. But, of course, the two roles are not mutually exclusive.

The non-executive director's role in big businesses in particular was well explored by the Cadbury Committee (set up in 1991) and in its report, as well as in the Hampel Review (1998), both of which gave guidance on corporate governance, and which ultimately influenced the drafting of the Combined Code. The Cadbury Committee tended to stress the corporate governance and 'policeman' benefits of a strong non-executive representation on a board, whereas the Hampel Review also emphasised the strategic thinking that non-executives can bring. Derek Higgs in his own influential review of the role of non-executives in 2003 noted that 'Non-executive directors are the custodians of the governance process.' But Higgs was also at pains to stress that the two roles should be seen as complementary rather than conflicting. He also rightly hinted that the excitement about the monitoring role owes perhaps something to the views of US regulators, 'who have tended to emphasise the monitoring role at the possible expense of the contribution the non-executive director can make to wealth creation'. For Higgs, an 'overemphasis on monitoring' will alienate a non-executive from the rest of the board. On the other hand, an 'overemphasis on strategy' risks undermining governance. It is an interesting trade-off bearing in mind a director's overall responsibilities, executive or non-executive. Nevertheless, the monitoring and accountability aspects of a board's performance are likely to dominate the role of the non-executive in a company with many external stakeholders – typically, therefore, the larger, publicly quoted company.

Smaller, owner-managed businesses might have to worry less about external stakeholders, but nevertheless they will still have stakeholders, and these will want to see that the company they do business with ensures their interests are dealt with appropriately. And I would argue that in all businesses the policing role should have an impact on strategy – indeed, if it is not interwoven into strategy delivery, the policing role is likely to be more honoured in the breach than in the observance. However, it is to be expected that non-executives will have a more direct influence on strategy on the boards of smaller, privately owned companies. The ways in which non-executives exercise this influence will vary, but the truth is that if non-executives do not have a strategic role they will not add value, and if they do not add value, they will not have a meaningful role at all.

The last executive/non-executive 'tendency' is the one that explores the tension between internal knowledge and external knowledge. Again, the area is both grey and contentious. As a part-timer with less experience of the business than the executives, a non-executive will therefore also have far less knowledge of its internal workings. On the other hand, a good non-executive will be able to bring to the board an awareness of the external context that will both compensate for his relative lack of knowledge of what is going on inside and enhance the overall capabilities of the board. However, it must be remembered that the non-executive is a director and is responsible for the company. Being part-time is an explanation but not an acceptable reason for ignorance.

Much focus has fallen recently on the role of the non-executive as steward of the interests of the shareholder, as it does every time shareholder value decreases across the board.

The assumption is that in a listed business there are occasions when the executive team is under pressure to forget who really owns the business and to whom the directors are ultimately accountable. There is also an assumption in this thinking that the shareholders in a listed business, regardless of their legal position, behave like owners. In owner-managed businesses board thinking – far from paying insufficient attention to its responsibility to shareholders – often fails to separate out shareholder issues from operational issues. An experienced non-executive will help an inexperienced management team ensure that shareholder issues and operational issues are discussed separately, using separate processes. Furthermore, as the company grows and the number of stakeholders increases, the executive team will rely on the non-executives more and more for ensuring that board processes evolve to reflect the issues and points of view that need to be tabled. Too many small businesses pay insufficient attention to the interests, for example, of minority shareholders who do not have board representation.

Non-executive tasks

Unsurprisingly, research would seem to show that there is a good corollary between a company's size (and complexity) and its enthusiasm for non-executives. One study for the Association of Chartered Certified Accountants suggested that the majority of small and medium-sized enterprises do not have a non-executive at all, and the proportion falls to as few as one in five for those businesses with fewer than 50 staff.[37] Nor can the same study find any connection between having a non-executive and improved financial performance – hardly a ringing endorsement. Yet there are some key non-executive roles to be performed even in younger, owner-managed businesses, roles that might be bundled and delivered by a non-executive director:

- Ensuring the board discharges its board functions properly, including supporting the chairman or managing director in boardroom discipline, keeping to the agenda and separating shareholder issues from operational issues.

- Contributing to and complementing management.

- Assisting the external growth of the business by helping it develop connections with customers, suppliers, financiers, industry contacts and so forth.

- Acting as a sounding board for executives when they are developing or revising strategy.

- Ensuring that when an objective view is needed, it is given. Important occasions are when directors' remuneration is to be discussed, when there is an issue raised by the auditors, and when recruiting a new director – but these are just examples. In big businesses some of them might be discharged by a committee of the board.

- Acting as a first point of review and challenge on management information – accounts, internal communications, press releases, business plans, strategy documents, etc.

- Providing counsel to the board and board members individually.

Items on this list of tasks are worth discussing in more detail. Firstly, with regard to ensuring the board works; without necessarily taking the role formally, a non-executive in a smaller business may well find himself taking a chairman-ship role, certainly helping ensure the business takes notice of governance issues as they begin to arise. 'I look for three key documents when I join the board,' a contact of mine with considerable non-executive experience with younger business observes:

> Firstly the accounts, so I can get to grips with the commercial reality and see if the executives can as well. Secondly, the strategic plan – there probably is not one, but creating one will tell the business a lot about where it wants to go and how it is going to get there. Thirdly, the organisation chart – again there probably will not be one of these, but the act of creating one will help sort out job roles, responsibilities and who reports to whom. I usually find that everyone is reporting to the MD, which is not a good starting point for decent governance or growth.

There are situations in the owner-managed business where a non-executive chair can be hugely advantageous. Family businesses in particular often have much to gain. Perhaps this is unsurprising: in many ways, a family business, sitting as it does on top of sets of sometimes conflicting and sometimes overlapping family issues and business issues, is similar to a big PLC, worried about managing its business and its shareholders. Specific instances include the transfer of the business from one family generation to another, and the appointment of 'joint managing directors' as an alternative to appointing one sibling or the other when neither is ready or interested. Even if not formally the chairman, a non-executive frequently has a facilitating role to play in the team leading the smaller business, ensuring a fair hearing is given to all important points of view, and no judgement escapes without a robust challenge.

Secondly on our list of tasks, the non-executive's main role in the smaller business is to complement and contribute to management and strategy. As the Hampel Review put it in 1998, it is 'Particularly in smaller companies [that] non-executive directors may contribute valuable experience not otherwise available to management'. In the smaller business it is not so much what the non-executive does to the board, or ensures that the board does, as what he brings to the board. The biggest barrier to growth in any younger business is the capacity of the senior management team. A non-executive can help provide valuable experience that may otherwise be in short supply. Besides, the essentials of the business model in the smaller business are likely to be simpler than in a big business, and thus somewhat easier for a part-time non-executive to grasp. The business will sell fewer products, and internal processes are likely to be simpler. A non-executive in a small business will be able to get closer to the day-to-day than in a big business.

Where is the boundary between executive and non-executive responsibility? This is more difficult to decide in theory than it is in practice. Although non-executives have to be careful to ensure that everyone knows there is a real distinction between being a non-executive and a part-time executive, clear reporting lines and de facto channels of command indicate to staff and others which members of the board really do have operational responsibilities. Non-executives, without direct people-management responsibilities and appearing on the premises only two or three times a month, are manifestly not in a position to exercise executive control. They are able to test the appropriateness of strategy, but their influence is necessarily exercised through the executives rather than around them. More serious is the issue of whether the non-executive has more influence on one member of the board than on another. Even if (inevitably) a non-executive will spend more time with some members of the board than others, she will be most effective in her role if she is available to the board as a whole and to all of its members. This is an independence issue, of course. Being closer to some board members than others can compromise a non-executive's effectiveness. Besides, as noted already, all directors have a duty to exercise independent judgement, and this includes independence from each other.

A non-executive director does not exercise influence just through the directors. Some of the non-executive's most important meetings are not board meetings and they take place outside the boardroom. There is a job to be done building (and occasionally repairing) bridges with suppliers, key customers, financiers, industry associations, competitors, regulators and so forth. Indeed, good non-executives are also well connected – in the sense, of course, of being well connected to the people that matter to the business. A non-executive director might or might not be the eyes and ears of the shareholders, but his eyes and ears are important nevertheless. Strategy and management are not just about command and control. They are far more about listening and learning. If you are close to decision making, there is a huge temptation to listen only to what you want to hear. A key role for a non-executive in a smaller business is to hear what needs to be heard, and then convert it, credibly, convincingly and persuasively, into what needs to be said.

The next point on our task list concerns the objective challenge. In addition to complementing management, a non-executive has a key role challenging management. I discuss board structure and the importance of challenge more later. Here I note that few issues exercise governance commentators more when a big company gets into trouble than whether the non-executives have provided a sufficient challenge to those taking the decisions that got the company into the mess in the first place. In a big business the audit committee – a committee of the board often comprised principally of non-executives – supervises the quality of financial reporting and provides an independent vehicle for managing the relationship with the external auditors, checking they do their job effectively, rigorously and efficiently, and ensuring that internal audit processes are sufficiently strong and recommendations acted on. Many smaller businesses are unlikely to have internal audit departments. Some of the smallest will not even be required statutorily to have an external audit. For many smaller businesses, it is a non-executive who provides the rudiments of an internal audit function, and notwithstanding the closeness of the management to the business and the relative simplicity of the stakeholder network, provides an independent eye and a critical review of processes and controls. Similarly, even if the business is not of a size to need a statutory external audit, there are stakeholders who will be keen to see the existence of external reviews and controls. The presence of a competent non-executive, along with an experienced and qualified finance director, may give comfort to potential suppliers and bankers for example. In big businesses, the non-executives form the cornerstones and capstones of the internal control and review processes, taking seats on the key committees.

Non-executive directors also have a key role in determining executives' remuneration. Questions were asked of the role of the non-executives at Royal Bank of Scotland in allowing CEO Sir Fred Goodwin to retire early on a pension of (initially at least) more than £700,000 after leading the bank to the brink of ruin. Most people have to rely on their bosses to determine their salary rise, but if you are the boss you have a splendid opportunity for abusing your own position. And if your business is funded in part at the expense of distant and independent shareholders, then you will be funding your decisions to your benefit at their expense. A key non-executive role in a listed business involves sitting on the remuneration committee, ensuring that the executives' remuneration is fair and appropriate. Once again, however, it is too easy to assume that there is no need for this role in a business where the executives and the shareholders are the same. Few issues are as divisive in the owner-managed business as the remuneration of members of the top team – even though, or perhaps especially, because it is the boss's decision. A non-executive has a useful role to play as referee and judge on these issues in even the smallest of businesses. The amounts may be smaller, but a small business is much more sensitive to the financial pressures brought by executive remuneration than most listed businesses. The remuneration packages of the chief executives of some ailing listed companies may continue to be woefully inappropriate notwithstanding the role of the non-executives, but even remuneration as considerable as that paid to Dick Fuld did not bring Lehman Brothers to its knees. This is not true of many owner-managed, entrepreneurial businesses, the owners of which have been only too willing to stake the healthy cash management of the business on a bonus for the directors or an overly generous dividend for the founders. An experienced non-executive can help ensure decisions like this are sensibly thought through rather than being bets thinly disguised under a veneer of commercial justification. A non-executive can also help ensure that the dividend policy is sensible – though a non-executive representing a venture capitalist, for example, is not necessarily going to be impartial.

Again, in a listed business it is important that processes for recruiting new directors – particularly a new chief executive – are objective and transparent, and hence the role of the nomination committee, and of the non-executives who sit on it. In smaller, private businesses, a non-executive also has much to add when the business is reviewing the performance of senior managers or planning to expand the top team. In particular, a non-executive can ensure that the selection process, which might otherwise be reduced to little more than a random assemblage of subjective judgements, is instead robust and objective. A non-executive can also ensure that the entrepreneur appreciates the importance of complementing the team, rather than finding someone to agree with him – in other words, someone who can help take the team towards the next stage of its evolution.

Recruiting non-executives

The recruitment of a non-executive director to a business is a challenge in itself. Some businesses do not have many options. As has already been noted, raising finance from a venture capitalist or a business angel for example often involves the VC or angel demanding a seat on the board. A business might expect a choice, although it should not expect too much of one. But even when the search for a non-executive is the company's own idea rather than someone else's, the choice may seem limited. The recruitment of all directors – but non-executives in particular – is one area of the economy where the free market seems to let everyone down, even in big businesses. If you believe some of those involved in finding non-executives, there is an acute shortage of decent candidates for the role of non-executive in big business. The statistics change from year to year, but research I reviewed for my book on non-executive directors in 2003 showed that 46 of the FTSE-100 companies shared at least one member of their remuneration committee with another FTSE-100 company, while just 392 directors made up the remuneration committees of 98 of the biggest UK companies, suggesting that the biggest non-executive jobs at least are shared by a relatively small number of individuals. The usual suspects seemed to be rather busy. Just 15 peers and MPs held 150 directorships, according to research by the *Financial Times,* and one leading Liberal Democrat held 21 directorships on his own. It is amazing he had any time for parliamentary business.[38] One could conclude from this concentration of so many directorships in the hands of so few, that there really are only very few who are up to the task, but there are other possible explanations too.

In fact there are lots of potential candidates interested in the role. The issue is not so much lack of supply as lack of definition. Increasing the pool of non-executives was a key concern identified by Derek Higgs in his 2003 review for the government of the role of non-executives. Indeed, Higgs suggested that the excitement about individuals holding too many directorships had been rather overdone in the interests of good copy. He also argued that the pool for potential non-executives was much larger than the one most frequently fished. He was right to contend that the supply could be helped by clarifying the role that non-executives are expected to fulfil, and a greater professionalism in the recruitment process itself. Many boards, in looking for a decent non-executive, are by no means sure what the role consists of. It is hardly surprising therefore that they do not know what sort of individual they are looking for. The easiest thing is for the successful candidate to define the role herself, and the most likely person to be able to define the role in your business is someone who is already fulfilling it in someone else's. No one, as the adage goes, got into trouble for buying from IBM. Until recently at least, no one got into trouble for recruiting a non-executive who was already a non-executive.

The lack of confidence in non-executive recruitment processes that afflicts big businesses, and which is founded essentially on ignorance, also afflicts small businesses. Indeed, the lack of confidence is even more marked in the smaller business. My experience suggests that younger owner-managed businesses are reluctant to turn to a register of non-executives or even to a specialist recruitment agency when looking to recruit, preferring instead to put their trust in family or friends. Often, of course, there is a cosy, self-fulfilling cycle here – for family businesses in particular. They want to keep the business in the family – and they are keen therefore to keep the family in the business, even if some parts of the family are reluctant. Maybe a non-executive role would be the best way to generate a bit of enthusiasm in an otherwise unenthusiastic family member.

The more forward-thinking younger businesses are most likely to turn to trusted professional sources for advice on potential non-executives. The accountant is a particularly popular port of call – more so nowadays than the bank manager, who is a creature of myth for an increasing number of smaller businesses. Research conducted by accountants BDO Stoy Hayward in winter 2002 suggested that of all external advisers, private company shareholders preferred to go to their accountants for advice. Indeed 31 per cent indicated their accountant as their preferred source of advice, compared to 24 per cent who preferred to call on a friend. Only 5 per cent indicated their lawyer, and 2 per cent their bank manager. Sources such as professional advisers are likely to have access to non-executives, as well as personal experience of them in action.

Non-executive positions have too often to date been filled by retired business people, or retired accountants and lawyers. To a certain extent this tendency is driven by perceptions of supply. In the 'good old days' the title indicated a sinecure rather than an active role, and now that the title does have a serious role to go with it, many are arguing that the job is too dangerous to be done by anyone other than the foolish. Whichever way you look at it, taking on the role of non-executive is hardly a good long-term career move. The role is usually part-time, and for a defined period of time, neither of which is likely to make the job more appealing to those facing the demands of bringing up a young family or dealing with a mortgage. Your non-executive – and everyone else's – will have to have a significant income from somewhere else, and have relatively low expectations for future career development. Retirees also have the advantage of having experience in abundance – and it is experience that is one of the most important things small businesses are looking for.

For many, however, a retired individual as non-executive sums up all that is wrong with thinking about board governance in recent years. Someone who is active as an executive elsewhere is far better qualified to act as a non-executive than a retiree, who may seem to be mainly after a supplement to their pension rather than the real challenges that non-executives have to deal with. So it is no surprise that in recent years there has been a shift from retirees to active executives as the best people to be non-executives. Indeed, one of Higgs's less-publicised recommendations was an 'invitation' to the chairmen of listed companies 'To encourage and facilitate their executive directors and suitable senior management just below board level to take one non-executive director position on a non-competitor board.'[39]

Looking for a non-executive in the pool of retired executives is not to be dismissed out of hand, however. For starters, 'retired' does not mean 'past it'. Among private companies in particular, there are capable individuals who, as a consequence of selling out, are looking for roles with meaning and challenge but without the commitment that goes with being an executive. In addition, executives active in small business management have not got the time to pay attention to a non-executive role elsewhere, and I'm a little surprised that Higgs thought that executives in listed companies do have such time. Besides, many of the qualities that you might look for in an executive you might think twice about in a non-executive. In an interesting article, seasoned non-executive Hamish Guthrie compared a typical advert for an executive with the response by the Institute of Chartered Accountants in England and Wales to Derek Higgs's call for consultation on the role of a decent non-executive.[40] A typical ad for an executive might read as follows: 'Action-orientated, strong focus on revenue and profit growth, motivational leader able to stretch the boundaries, team player to drive change and deliver against challenging strategy and targets ...' On the other hand, Guthrie quotes from the ICAEW's response to the Higgs Review: 'Independent of mind, with honesty and integrity, curiosity and willingness to challenge results even when they appear to be successful, willing to stand up to executive directors and, if appropriate resign.' There is indeed a fundamental mismatch here, but not really one between 'retired' and 'active' – more one between the sorts of individuals that are needed on successful boards and how they fit together.

Nonetheless, there are executives who would work well as non-executives, and Higgs's recommendations might well foster interest in the area to the particular advantage of smaller businesses. On the face of it there is a lot that is attractive in this idea. Senior managers in big businesses are often tempted by the prospect of a directorship somewhere else. Indeed, such experience may better prepare them for future roles in their current businesses. On the other hand, smaller businesses often look to their non-executives for help building the controls and management infrastructure needed for the bigger business they hope to become. Additionally, a big business is more likely than a small business to be able to flex the workload of its senior management and make the prospect of someone taking on a non-executive directorship sensible. Whether the idea becomes a reality or not remains to be seen. Certainly, for all the good reasons in favour of the idea, there are plenty of problems – not least conflicts of time and interest.

It is important when recruiting a non-executive to carefully define the qualities you are looking for, and to expect (indeed demand) that they are different from those you see in your executives. (Some CEOs will always make poor non-executives as they will always find it difficult, if not impossible, to relinquish the chief executive role even when not appointed to it.) As with all new board appointments to a growing, entrepreneurial business, a new non-executive has to add to the board rather than merely reinforce it. The following list might do for starters:

- Broad business experience, not restricted to the sector or the size of business you are in.

- The ability to assess people and situations analytically and dispassionately.

- The ability to hold one's ground, but also the ability to persuade others of one's own point of view.

- Financial literacy – able to read, write, understand and speak the languages of corporate finance and management accounting.

- Awareness of the legal environment and the duties and obligations owed to other parties and stakeholders, both by the directors and the company.

- Familiarity with best board practice, and how this might be interpreted for a business the size of yours.

- The ability to act as a sounding board for other directors, which implies approachability as well as first-class interpersonal and communication skills – in particular an ability to listen and understand.

- Experience of the industry in which you operate, in addition to general business experience.

- A sense of humour.

- A sense of humility – particularly if they are experienced executives in their own right.

The personal skills listed here are even more important than the technical ones, and are certainly more difficult to identify in a recruitment process. Derek Higgs in his report on the role of non-executives in listed businesses summed up these personal qualities excellently: 'Non-executive directors need to be sound in judgement and to have an inquiring mind. They should question intelligently, debate constructively, challenge rigorously and decide dispassionately. And they should listen sensitively.'[41]

Before closing this section it is important to stress that the relationship between a non-executive and her company should be documented. The document is unlikely to be an employment contract because the individual is unlikely to be an employee, but it will state the duties the non-executive is expected to discharge, in return for what package. Documentation should also be drafted that defines the relationship between the non-executive and the executive and the board – defining and circumscribing the respective duties of each to their business and to each other, as well as defining the types of decisions that need to be referred to whom. As with all spheres of business life, the more duties can be defined and documented, the more business risks can be managed – particularly given that the role of non-executive continues to be hazily defined in law. And the role of non-executive, in businesses both big or small, is nothing if not increasingly risky.

Finance directors in particular

Although by and large statute, regulation and guidance are silent on the subject, the role of finance director is a special one on the board and has a particular place in any governance framework.

The finance director's seat on the board is well established – more established than that of the independent chairman, for example. When young businesses mature and start taking governance seriously they are more likely to appoint a decent finance director than they are to appoint a chairman or even a non-executive director. Many are the businesses in which the human resources director or marketing director, notwithstanding their directorial titles, do not actually have seats on the board. This is rarely true of the finance director. Before putting in money, financial investors will want to ensure their money is in good hands, and a key piece of evidence is the presence of a finance director with the appropriate qualifications and experience. The finance director will be the first line of defence inside the business against poor financial decisions – and, of course, financial impropriety. He or she will also be the first check and balance on the ambitions of the chief executive – earlier even than the non-executives. Lloyd Dorfman, when Chief Executive of Travelex, noted that before deciding on a matter of strategic importance, he used to put it through his operations director and his finance director, both long-standing team members, confident that they would give him and his plans a thorough going over.[42] If he still wanted to proceed after the 'going over', it was probably still worth doing.

Unsurprisingly, the finance director has been described by at least one chief executive as 'the man who likes to say "no!"' On the other hand, as noted elsewhere, the finance director in many businesses is the chief executive's heir apparent – the inference being that it is the finance director who is closest to all the decisions that matter. Being able to maintain a due sense of distance from the other executives in the interests of good governance is thus an important quality in a finance director, but one not easily achieved. Too many finance directors are rightfully criticised by their CEOs for not contributing sufficiently to the evolution of strategy in the business. But a finance director who is too close to strategy formation will not be able to be objective about it.

In many organisations the finance director quite often is the only member of the board with a professional qualification and the individual most likely to be briefed on corporate governance. The finance director is certainly the individual likely to have to deal with those provisions of governance that are imposed by external agencies. It is no coincidence that the Combined Code is published by the Financial Reporting Council, which describes itself as 'the UK's independent regulator responsible for promoting confidence in corporate reporting and governance'. The finance director, notwithstanding the existence of an audit committee, will be the primary point of contact with the company's auditors. He is also most likely to be the individual responsible for setting up the organisation's internal control systems.

When governance breaks down one of the first questions to be asked – in addition to 'Where were the non-execs?' – is 'Where was the finance director?' Chief executives or other senior officials who have things to hide only stand a chance of doing so convincingly with the connivance, negligence or incompetence of the finance director. The finance director is responsible for the machinery that generates the financial reports and accounts, the means by which the directors tell the story of the business and its performance to the outside world. Andrew Fastow, erstwhile Chief Financial Officer of Enron, was widely credited (perhaps not the right word) with the complex structures established by Enron to help conceal its losses. Fastow – the holder of an MBA, but not a chartered accountant or CPA – was, at the time of writing, serving his sentence after pleading guilty to two counts of wire and securities fraud. Previously he was indicted by a federal grand jury on 78 counts including fraud, money laundering and conspiracy. Fastow was not solely responsible for the disaster that was Enron, but it cannot be imagined without him. WorldCom's demise was widely blamed on its Chief Executive, Bernie Ebbers, but Chief Financial Officer Scott Sullivan, after testifying against Ebbers in the witness box, was sentenced to five years in prison after being found guilty on three counts of securities fraud. The sentencing judge described Sullivan as the 'architect' of the fraud.

Systemic corporate governance failures almost always involve at their heart a finance director who is either incompetent or acting inappropriately. Sullivan and Fastow were both too close to the business and too close to their CEOs in order to be able to assess the strategies their companies were pursuing with anything other than conflicted eyes. Certainly in the case of Enron the finance director took the auditors too close to the company as well. The financial controls that should have been in place, and that should have been the responsibility of the finance director, would have helped prevent the excesses from happening in the first place. The transparency and lines of communication I discuss elsewhere in this book, if they had been working properly in Enron and WorldCom, would have at least shone the light of day on some critically important areas of the business, and thus offered concerned parties – directors, regulators, shareholders, customers – a better chance of doing something about it. Transparency and lines of communication and the stories, good and bad, that pass along them, are also key responsibilities of the finance director.

Entrepreneurs

Entrepreneurs and governance do not fit well together, as the paragraphs above about Stelios Haji-Iannou, Richard Branson, Anita Roddick and more illustrate. Too often governance is seen as an antidote to entrepreneurship. This is a pity – both for entrepreneurs and for governance. The entrepreneurial instinct is the catalyst for change, growth and success at the heart of businesses big and small. A system of governance that constrains, ignores or destroys entrepreneurship is a system that sows the seeds of its own destruction. Nonetheless, entrepreneurship has always been a dirty word in some parts of the world. The trouble with the French, George Bush is supposed to have observed, is that they do not have a word for entrepreneur. When economies turn sour and good business ideas turn bad, the entrepreneurial heroes of one part of the cycle turn into the villains of the next. This is unfair on entrepreneurs. Bernard Madoff's alleged villainy stretched back long before he confessed to it, and most entrepreneurs would struggle in accepting him as one of their own. Governance, on the other hand, might have a role containing the excesses of entrepreneurship, but then it has a role controlling excesses full stop.

Corporate governance would deal with entrepreneurship better if entrepreneurship was itself better understood. Experimental evidence suggests that, statistically, individuals are more likely to take a risk to avoid a loss rather than to realise a gain.[43] In other words, most individuals are more likely to worry about last year's mistake than next year's opportunity. Interestingly, notwithstanding this bias, it has been demonstrated that neither approach is inherently more risky than the other. Perhaps there is something in the entrepreneurial make-up that reverses this typical attitude to risk. Certainly in my experience, entrepreneurs look forwards rather than backwards. It is not that an entrepreneurial venture is necessarily inherently more risky or more in need of careful oversight from the priests of governance – rather it is that many an entrepreneur evaluates the risk differently. If this hypothesis is right, it points to a marked contrast in the approach to risk between someone with an entrepreneurial mindset and individuals with a more typical approach such as a finance director, or a non-executive, or a chairman. Accountants, let us not forget, are trained for at least three years to create complex financial reports that describe the past and are often out of date even before they are published.

To be fair, the Combined Code recognises that entrepreneurship has a key role to play and governance has some sort of responsibility for it, or at least relation to it. The opening words of the Code state:

> Good corporate governance should contribute to better
> company performance by helping a board discharge
> its duties in the best interests of shareholders; if it is
> ignored, the consequence may well be vulnerability or
> poor performance. Good governance should facilitate
> efficient, effective *and entrepreneurial* [my italics]
> management that can deliver shareholder value over
> the longer term. The Combined Code on Corporate
> Governance ... is published by the FRC to support these
> outcomes and promote confidence in corporate reporting
> and governance.

The word 'entrepreneurial' to my ear reads a little like an afterthought, as does the last phrase about corporate reporting and governance. But it is good to see them in the same paragraph.

The best way of reconciling governance and entrepreneurship is to see them not in opposition but as pulling in the same direction. Julian Metcalfe's words on his partner Sinclair Beecham are worth quoting again: 'Without me the business would not be there, and without him it would not work.' Successful business teams are comprised of people with very different skills and outlooks who nonetheless are prepared to and succeed in working with each other for the common good of the company. Working together is easy if you all think the same way, but unlikely to lead to as robust decision taking as the product of two or minds who think differently. 'When two people in business agree, one of them is unnecessary,' William Wrigley of chewing gum fame once remarked. Governance at its best successfully reconciles different points of view, and one of those different points of view in business has to be the entrepreneurial. At its worst governance ensures the tidy and efficient dictatorship of one point of view. The weak 'single-mindedness' that is akin to dictatorship is at the heart of many governance failings: if the non-executives had been more challenging and the executives more challenged, perhaps the disaster that was Enron might not have happened.

Partners

Partnerships are what happen when more than one sole trader gets together, and they all want to be principals in the business. Essentially partnerships have all the disadvantages of sole traders, with some inevitable extra complications of scale thrown in. But it is not just scale creating the particular governance problems that partnerships need to address. Partnerships have unique characteristics that need recognising and addressing in governance mechanisms. Not infrequently, partners are tempted to think of their organisations as limited companies, and to presume that the governance mechanisms that suit companies are the solutions to the governance problems of partnership. In several important ways this line of thinking is mistaken.

Partners, like their organisations, in several ways are unusual animals, and are both different from and similar to staff, directors and shareholders. First, partners, like sole traders, are 'self-employed', which gives some tax advantages; but like sole traders, partners in a traditional partnership also have unlimited liability. Indeed, they are jointly and severally liable for each other's liabilities, with the actions of one partner conceivably leading to the personal financial ruin of any or all of the other partners. Awareness of personal unlimited liability is pressure enough; but responsibility for the liability of partners as well is qualitatively as well as quantitatively distinctive. The development of the Limited Liability Partnership potentially changes this dynamic – but not necessarily for the better.

Partners, like sole traders, as owner-managers are also responsible for financing their organisations. Although there are examples of partnerships that have tapped the bond market, it remains relatively difficult for partnerships, even quite substantial partnerships, to raise external finance, and the partnership's finance-raising capacity is essentially the same as the sum of the individual capacities of the partners. Partners are the principal source, therefore, of a partnership's capital.

Partners are individuals, and they have different attitudes and abilities – different abilities to be harnessed when generating profits for the business, and different attitudes to putting money into the business. Differences such as these (and there are more of course) put pressure on the relationships between partner and partner, as well as between the partners and the businesses for which they are responsible. Relationships between different types of stakeholder are always asymmetrical, but in partnerships the asymmetry is peculiar because the most important asymmetry is between different classes of worker, and not between insiders and outsiders. Good governance in partnerships sets out not just to protect outsiders from insiders, or the suppliers of capital from managers, but partners from themselves and each other.

Governance for partnerships starts with legislation – and ancient legislation at that. The Partnership Act of 1890 offers a safety net of legislation to protect from themselves those partnerships that have chosen not to tailor partnership agreements to govern their own affairs. The Act sets a baseline for 'hygiene' matters such as internal financial reporting timetables, but also rules on some significant issues; for example, that the partnership will automatically dissolve in the event of a partner leaving, which can be quite a nuisance. (A partnership wishing to get round this one, and some of the other provisions of the Act, will need to draft its own partnership agreement.) Things have changed a lot in business since 1890. In particular, business has got much more complicated, and the organisational resources required to solve the problems business presents have demanded larger and more complicated organisations. The 1890 Act was written for a smaller, more intimate, more personal world. (Indeed, until relatively recently partnerships were restricted in size to 20 partners.) But the very fact that partnerships are still governed by a piece of legislation that dates from the century before last (consultation on revisions has been going on for at least 10 years) suggests that, as a mechanism for sharing ownership, and for establishing a well-balanced commercial entity, the partnership, for all its drawbacks, has been hugely successful.

In part the success of partnerships, measured by longevity at least, has been a matter of regulation. Many professionals, lawyers and accountants in particular, have been *obliged* by professional regulations to practise as partnerships regardless of any commercial or personal desire to incorporate. In recent years there has been plenty of yearning, by accountants in particular, for the haven of incorporation and the limited liability status that this offers its owners. In a more and more litigious environment, unlimited liability is considered to be very risky. Insurance cover, which to some extent reduces the risks, has become increasingly expensive and has offered unsatisfactory protection. Ever since the statutory limit of 20 on the number of partners in a partnership was relaxed for certain types of partnership, many large partnerships have felt less like partnerships and more like incorporated entities anyway. Likewise, many of the partners in a 2,000-partner partnership have felt more like employees than partners.

If you are beginning to look and feel like an incorporated corporation, why not become one? The Limited Liability Partnership (not to be confused with the Limited Partnership) has been invented as a compromise to allow partners in partnerships, while retaining some of the benefits of unincorporation (including tax benefits), to enjoy some of the protection allowed to the owners of limited companies in return for a requirement to file audited financial information. 'LLP' status, governed by the Limited Liability Partnership Act of 2000, gives to a partnership an identity separate from its partners, though in many ways this is giving legal recognition to what for some partners has substantially been the case anyway. More importantly, LLP status grants to individual partners significant protection from the liabilities of their partners.

The recent evolution of the LLP does not prove that partnerships will turn into standard limited corporations after all, or that the partnership model itself is dead. Far from it. There are good reasons why partnerships work. No business structure fosters a closer bond between the owners and the substance of the business itself. You can think of it as a manifestation of the old 'gentlemen's club' if you wish, but being a partner in a partnership does give a curious sense of belonging, ownership and shared commitment that, notwithstanding fancy talk about 'brand' and 'culture' and 'values', corporates sometimes struggle hard to emulate. For years, large limited companies have sought to reduce their layers of middle management and empower a more flexible and flatter, networked structure of senior individuals, but partnerships have had no need to – they have been there all the time.

Volunteers

The role of volunteers in organisations, and their consequences for governance, is often underestimated. Typically, the individuals who sit on the boards of charities and other types of social enterprise are not paid for their services. Indeed this is a fundamental characteristic of charity governance. Many trustees refuse even to reclaim out-of-pocket expenses. Many social enterprises – charities in particular – formally name their boards of directors boards of trustees, or boards of governors. Just like directors in companies, boards of trustees are responsible for the overall supervision of the organisation. Their responsibilities are the same as those of their peers in commercial enterprises. In large charities trustees will often act in a non-executive capacity only – the organisation that they lead will be managed by a salaried management team. In such an organisation even the senior financial officer – the treasurer – usually acts in an 'honorary' capacity, and it is a senior salaried financial officer who runs the accounting function, reporting to the unpaid trustees. But it is the honorary treasurer who, as trustee, will carry the can. Smaller charities are led, managed and staffed by volunteers.

Governance in the social enterprise sector is evolving. One of the characteristics of Community Interest Companies (CICs), a new, hybrid vehicle designed to cater for the new world of 'social entrepreneurship', is their ability to pay their directors – but even here, I suggest, CIC directors, paid or not, will see themselves more as trustees than directors. The very label 'trustee' is interesting and meaningful. The trustees of a charity are in effect its directors, and are responsible for its direction; but the notion of 'trusteeship' suggests that they are responsible for the safeguarding and stewardship of assets for the benefit of individuals other than themselves. This is a conception of the role of director that directors of many for-profit organisations might learn from.

Social enterprises, big and small, compared to with-profit organisations, are therefore much more likely to benefit from the services of volunteers who are not trustees, working alongside, and often in lieu of, paid staff. Volunteers present an entirely different challenge from salaried employees to managers and to the makers of governance frameworks. Volunteers offer their services for a wide variety of reasons, mostly very personal to the individual. Yes, there will usually be some consonance with the objectives of the social enterprise itself (though this may be quite remote!), but quite often volunteers will think very differently from each other, and their thoughts and feelings will be held and defended with a passion that will on occasion take by surprise managers new to the sector and previously used only to salaried employees. Because volunteers are not paid they can be difficult for the organisation for whom they do such valuable service to manage or influence. Volunteers can be more difficult to reach, let alone measure. Social enterprises often cannot say with any degree of certainty where their volunteers come from, why they do what they do, what they do, or even how many they have. Attempts to survey them can often fail. Although it is easy for a wealthy charity to organise a conference or workshop, they will not know whether volunteers will turn up. Volunteers are giving up their own time after all.

Volunteers are also often suspicious of any corporate-style activity. Such activity will cost time and resource which might otherwise be devoted to the objects of the social enterprise. Tensions between volunteers and salaried officials are almost inevitable. Volunteers give of their time and their own money to further the social enterprise's aims. But salaried staff have to be paid just to turn up. The fact that salaries paid by social enterprises are often below those paid in 'commercial' organisations will cut little ice with some volunteers. Volunteers are often suspicious of the efforts of any head office, and in large, multi-site social enterprises, volunteers will owe their loyalties often to the corner of the organisation they work for. Head office in turn will often find itself frustrated by its volunteers, and its own seeming inability to exercise serious leverage over them. Some will dream how much easier life would be without volunteers, but most wake up to the reality that their organisation would not function without them.

Interestingly, the governance issues presented to social enterprises by volunteers are beginning to be confronted by organisations seeking to make a profit. It is increasingly far too simplistic to assume that staff will respond to carrot and stick just because they are paid. Particularly valuable and particularly well-paid staff have always tended to sit outside the performance management regime. I have come across well-paid executives more than prepared to flout an organisation's chosen strategy and to risk losing an element of bonus for reasons of personal motivation, rational or otherwise. Of course, the highest-paid staff can afford the luxury of disobedience, albeit within limits. But increasingly even junior staff are inclined to behave in ways more typical of volunteers than paid employees, putting work–life balance, or environmental concerns, higher up their list of concerns than money when working for an organisation regardless of sector. To some thinkers about governance this might be seen as a challenge; others will see the consequent role given to values and principles as an opportunity.

5 | Stakeholders

'To trust people is a luxury in which only the wealthy can indulge; the poor cannot afford it.'

E. M. Forster[44]

Much corporate governance thinking has agency theory as its fundamental premise – that management acts as agent for the owner; that the interests of management and owner conflict, and that there are costs to be incurred if owners wish to monitor let alone align managers. Agency theory has implications for rule-making, for reward and incentive mechanisms, and for assumptions about culture, control and hierarchy. But there are alternative foundations on which to base governance frameworks, some of which have already been alluded to.

Stakeholder theory has been described, not entirely favourably, as, 'a conceptual cocktail, concocted from a variety of disciplines and producing a blend of appealing sociological and organisational flavours'.[45] In essence, stakeholder theory seeks to recognise the importance in a business of stakeholders other than the owners and managers. Stakeholders might not have shares but they will nonetheless have an interest in the organisation. Attempts to compare and contrast agency and stakeholder theory note the simplicity of the former and the complexity of the latter. Agency theory has also been seen as decidedly old-fashioned, whereas stakeholder theory reaches to a more inclusive, pluralist, modern conception of the purpose and functioning of an organisation. A classic definition of a company describes it as 'an island of managerial control in a sea of market relations'.[46] Harvard professor Joseph Badaracco describes this, in comparison with more multi-faceted approaches to management, as:

> Badly out of date ... In reality most firms are now enmeshed in networks of ongoing relationships. Strategic alliances link firms with their customers and suppliers, and sometimes with labour unions, governments, university laboratories, and even competitors. Many companies also have complicated dealings with the media, government regulators, local communities, and various interest groups.[47]

The list is not exclusive, of course. I would add families of employees for starters, and banks in 2009 would add their competitors – recognising that the world of finance is now tightly interlocked, and what happens to one bank in one corner of the world will have ramifications for another bank in another corner. In a multi-stakeholder world, many stakeholders will have several hats. The company at the middle of a stakeholder network can be forgiven for being confused when many of its stakeholders are not sure which hat they are wearing today. Indeed, companies will have stakeholders they did not even know existed until some crisis or opportunity brings them to the surface. Certainly the credit crunch has brought all sorts of stakeholders to the attention of the banks that they have previously either chosen to ignore or did not know existed in the first place. Even when taking account of the stakeholders the company is aware of, stakeholder theory attempts to account for a much more complicated picture of the corporate world than agency theory with its dualistic obsession with managers and shareholders.

Agency theory and stakeholder theory are at one and the same time so close to each other and so far apart. Stakeholders of all persuasions will look to management as their agents in the organisation in which they have an interest. But management, if trying to satisfy the concerns of all stakeholders, will find itself in an impossible position. Management can define its position, or 'align itself' relatively easily with reference to just one stakeholder, but not when there are many. Indeed, a stakeholder theory approach to governance reminds regulators and regulated that business decision taking is about taking difficult choices; balancing the interests of stakeholders who compete and complement each other untidily. Of course, in satisfying the objectives of one set of stakeholders at the expense of another, management are inviting the disaffected group to cry that the management are merely misaligned agents. When governance fails, however, many if not all sets of stakeholders suffer. The Enron disaster is an interesting case in point. Given that it was ultimately the shareholders who lost their money when the company went under it could be argued that management interests were insufficiently aligned with those of the shareholders. But in many ways the problem at the heart of Enron was the lack of regard management paid to any stakeholders other than themselves. One set of commentators observes that:

> The catastrophe caused by the failure of Enron, could
> not compare with the damage this company would have
> caused if it had succeeded ... [I]f Enron had continued
> to succeed making ever-rising profits by amoral means,
> exploiting business strategies that wreaked havoc in
> the economies they operated in, then shareholders'

interests may have been served with the denial of every
other conceivable economic interest as the company
continued to hike prices by exercising monopoly power,
destabilising essential energy and other services, creating
volatility in markets that undermined the prospects of
continuing normal business in other industries, and
damaging people's lives as a result ... Enron not only
betrayed its shareholders, in a more immediate and
direct way it betrayed its customers, and in the end its
employees also.[48]

Given that the catastrophe ended up with criminal convictions for several of its directors and executives, and destroyed its audit firm, the officers of the company ultimately did not fare well out of the story either.

Recognising the existence and interests of stakeholders asks much more from corporate governance than a simple shareholder–manager alignment approach allows. The multifarious demands of different stakeholders inevitably force managers back to first principles and statements of guidance rather than specific rules, which will be impossible to design to meet the diverse and contradictory interests of all. Stakeholders cannot be expected to agree with each other, let alone be able to present a common set of issues for the regulators to rationalise.

Under this approach to governance, trust and good faith, people skills, persuasion and negotiation have a much more powerful role to play than the application of rules, or even the pursuit of 'alignment'. Agency theory implies the worst of people's motives, and if you assume the worst of people when you design your control frameworks and incentive mechanisms, you should not be surprised when you get it. The more stakeholders there are the more complicated the governance agenda, and the more it needs to be addressed by an armoury of soft tools, and the more the outcome is likely to need to be characterised by balance, fairness and compromise. A stakeholder-focused approach to governance inevitably puts more pressure on personal behaviour and responsibility, and it therefore inevitably brings with it a political agenda. As two US professors have put it: 'To get what they want in law and regulation ... these actors must move disagreements inside the firm out and into the public arena. To obtain their preferred corporate governance outcome, they have to win in politics.'[49]

Notwithstanding the difficulties, a stakeholder-driven political approach to governance is increasingly the approach that companies are having to face up to. Gary Hamel, London Business School professor, and business guru, wrote in February 2009 that we need to 'fully embed the ideas of community and citizenship in management systems'. He continued:

> [T]oday, corporate governance structures often exacerbate conflict by promoting the interests of some groups – like senior executives and the providers of capital – at the expense of others – usually employees and local communities. In the future, management systems must reflect the ethos of community and citizenship, thereby recognising the interdependence of all stakeholder groups.[50]

Even before the credit crunch, lots of US states passed laws permitting or even requiring directors to consider the impact of their actions on stakeholders other than shareholders. The deepening economic crisis will exacerbate things further.

As has already been noted, there are of course many organisations that do not have shareholders at all. Many, though by no means all, social enterprises do not have shareholders – and even if they do have 'owners' of some sort, they stand in very different relation to their organisations than the shareholders of for-profit companies. But social enterprises do have stakeholders. First and perhaps foremost are the donors who provide much of the finance. Donors to a charity will not be shareholders in it, not will they expect to be, but they will have a keen interest in what happens to the money they give. Charities worry rightly about what proportion of the money given to them is spent on administration. Their finance directors take careful note of whether funds have been donated with specific projects in mind, and therefore have to be ring-fenced for those projects only. (This can be a particular headache when the project changes or disappears, but the charity still has the money in its bank account.)

In addition to donors there are the individuals intended as the beneficiaries of the organisation's endeavours. It is a mistake to assume that such individuals stand in the same relation to the social enterprise as customers do to a company. To start off with, many of the beneficiaries of a social enterprise do not seek the service or money that is their due, and when they receive it they do not necessarily know, owing perhaps to incapacity, where it comes from. Sometimes the ultimate beneficiaries of a social enterprise, certainly one involved in animal welfare, aren't even human. The individuals who give social enterprises and charities money do not just include donors, they also include beneficiaries. Charities rarely benefit from paying 'customers' – at least not directly. Unsurprisingly, governance arrangements for charities necessarily are as sophisticated as those for listed companies, and have a far longer pedigree. In great part this is because they have long recognised the complexity of the web of stakeholder interests in which they are set and on which they depend.

6 Rules and codes

'Laws are partly formed for the sake of good men in order to instruct them how they may live on friendly terms with one another, and partly for the sake of those who refuse to be instructed, whose spirit cannot be subdued, or softened, or hindered from plunging into evil.'

Plato

As economic history has demonstrated, when the booms that precede the inevitable crashes are at their peak, greed and self-interest are shown only too often to be more powerful and compelling than reason and self-restraint. Humankind it seems cannot be left to its own devices if the aim is sustained economic stability. The governance arrangements that support sustained economic stability cannot just be left to people or good intentions either. Externally imposed rules and regulations, which seek to push organisations and the people that are involved in them into ways of behaviour that minimise the consequences of greed and protect against self-interest, are drafted to plug the gap.

F.D. Roosevelt had no doubt in his mind about the role regulation – or rather the lack of it – played in the 1929 crash and the ensuing depression. 'We require ... safeguards against a return of the evils of the old order; there must be a strict supervision of all banking and credits and investments.' For 'strict supervision' read rules and a regulatory system, which his government set about establishing, not just for Wall Street but also for other areas of economic activity. The Glass-Steagall Act of 1933 amongst other things prohibited investment bankers betting deposits on the buying and selling of tradable financial securities, in effect separating banking and investment banking. The Securities and Exchange Commission (SEC), created in 1934, was also a product of Roosevelt's administration, designed to address the free-market anarchy that existed in the run-up to the Wall Street Crash, used so cynically by sophisticated investors to further their own interests, at the expense of less knowledgeable and more distant investors who were often their customers and clients. Perhaps even more interesting, bearing in mind the future evolution of Enron, was the Public Utility Holding Company Act of 1935, aimed at financial structures – principally structures of companies concentrated in holding companies, which in effect to that date had ensured control of public utilities remained with Wall Street financiers. The Act stated that the utility companies should voluntarily get rid of those holding companies that had no useful function, but should this not be carried through within five years (by 1 January 1940) the SEC 'would be empowered to compel the dissolution of every holding company which did not establish an economic reason for its existence'. Title II of the Act authorised the Federal Power Commission to integrate the utility operating companies into regional systems on the basis of technical efficiency, not speculative manipulation, thus aiming another blow at financiers seeking to secure their own self-interest rather than that of those looking for fuel and water.

It is more than ironic to note how many of Roosevelt's regulations and rules introduced in the 1930s were relaxed and repealed in the last decades of the 20th century – when they apparently were no longer needed. The Big Bang in the City of London in 1986 was one of the most important moves towards deregulation, followed in 1987 by a relaxation in the US of the Glass-Steagall prohibitions against bank deposits being used for investment banking, relaxed further in 1996 and abolished altogether in 1999. Indeed, the bull market leading up to the crash of 2008 ran parallel to a fashion for deregulation sponsored by successive administrations culminating in those led by George W. Bush and Gordon Brown. That Barack Obama's campaign for the presidency once again included calls for re-regulation and regulatory reform suggests that the cycles of regulation and deregulation, and boom, bust and stability, move in contrary directions.

Nonetheless, notwithstanding the attempts of the deregulators, 2009 is a very different world from 1929, and for many, if not most, corporate governance is still all about rules and only rules. Unsurprisingly, the starting point for most people looking to find out more about governance is the relevant rulebook. Find out the rulebook that applies to you, and ensure that you comply as efficiently and effectively as possible. If your organisation changes this might well have the effect of promoting or demoting you from one set of rules to another, or indeed out of the scope of a rulebook altogether.

The UK Combined Code – a principles-based approach

As has already been seen, for some individuals, escaping from governance regulations is a driver of organisational change rather than a consequence of it. Indeed the deregulators have always had supporters, and governance and the notion of the rulebook had an uncomfortable relationship after 1929 and before. Too much regulation, just like too little, will kill the enterprise on which all economic activity depends. The best-known formulation of governance principles in the UK is the Combined Code, which was first issued in 1998 and has been updated at regular intervals since then. The June 2008 edition applies to accounting periods beginning on or after 29 June 2008. I discuss the practical implications of the Code in more detail elsewhere in this book. For the time being I consider it as an example of governance as a set of rules – although, famously, one thing the Combined Code is *not* is a set of rules. An early paragraph explains:

> The Code is not a rigid set of rules. Rather, it is a guide to the components of good board practice distilled from consultation and widespread experience over many years. While it is expected that companies will comply wholly or substantially with its provisions, it is recognised that non-compliance may be justified in particular circumstances if good governance can be achieved by other means. A condition of non-compliance is that the reasons for it should be explained to shareholders, who may wish to discuss the position with the company and whose voting intentions may be influenced as a result. This 'comply or explain' approach has been in operation since the Code's beginnings in 1992 and the flexibility it offers is valued by company boards and by investors in pursuing better corporate governance.[51]

It is worth exploring the implications of this approach. No, the Combined Code does not set out rules as normally understood – after all, every organisation to which the Code applies is given the opportunity to exempt itself from any of its provisions. However, the requirement to explain yourself if you do not comply has the consequence of presenting such explanations as confessions of guilt. Certainly, as has already been seen, organisations that choose to explain rather than comply often get rough treatment in the press and from outsiders – even from institutional investors. The consequences of failing to comply are thus serious – perhaps more serious than any punishment that might be meted out by a regulator seeking to deal with an organisation that breaks a rule. However, explaining non-compliance with a principle is a different matter from deliberately or even accidentally breaking a rule. Conversely, drafting a principle the breach of which might be explained away is very different from drafting a rule the breach of which will need to give rise to punishment. Further, there are good reasons why a principle-based approach to governance is much more attractive than a rule-based approach.

Complexity

Rules always struggle with the complexity that is reality. For rules to reflect the detail of that complexity they themselves need to be complicated. Complication adds to expense when drafting, interpreting and applying rules. A thick rulebook needs reading by people in your business who understand what they are reading, and who are sufficiently authoritative within the business to be able to effect the changes required to comply. The alternative to complexity is to prescribe rules that deal with generalities only. But rulebooks that deal in the general end up inevitably being tissues of loopholes, which inevitably are construed as invitations to break the rules by those the rules were designed to constrain in the first place. On the other hand, rulebooks that attempt to capture the complexity of reality themselves inevitably fall foul of the loophole facility as well. Indeed, the more precise the rules the more likely it is they will fail to cater for every eventuality, and a hole caused by oversight in a rulebook that aims at covering every eventuality looks a lot bigger than a loophole to anyone minded to sidetrack the rules. General rulebooks might be tissues of loopholes; specific rulebooks are universes with black holes.

Either way, detailed or general, rules and regulations throw down an implicit challenge to the directors – 'See if you can find a way past us.' On the other hand, guidance and recommendation throws down a different but surely healthier challenge to the directors: 'Look – we've thought about this long and hard, but we do not expect to be perfect; indeed we do not think it is even possible to draft the perfect rulebook. So if you have a case for not complying, that's fine, but tell the world what your case is, and let the world judge whether your case is acceptable; whether you have genuinely identified a situation we did not envisage, or if you are just looking for any excuse not to comply with good practice.' Guidance and recommendation, therefore, is much more likely than rule and regulation to foster a culture of honesty. Guidelines are rules for responsible grown-ups. Rules are what you have to fall back on for governing the irresponsible.

Enforcement

Rules are worthless unless people comply, but enforcement is difficult. To ensure compliance you need enforcement mechanisms – inspectors, judges, punishments. The more complicated the rules the more enforcement mechanisms are required. Faced with regulatory complexity some businesses, particularly small businesses, just surrender. If you do not understand, or haven't got the time or resources to consider and comply, you do nothing, hoping that you will be alright, or if not, then you will not be the one who is found out.

Unfortunately this is the situation in the UK with employment legislation. Many management teams of small businesses in particular would be hard pressed to comment authoritatively on whether their businesses comply with the detailed prescriptions of employment legislation, and they will only face up to the detail when an employee sues for constructive dismissal on the basis of a sin the company never knew it had committed in the first place. Enforcement-based governance is inherently reactionary, therefore, and driven by the threat of punishment, which in turn makes it unpopular, and can even tend towards making heroes out of those who get caught up by it. In many cases, the threat of punishment is far from threatening. Regulators without good eyes to see evil when it is being committed, and without real teeth to ensure their sanctions have influence, are useless, as is any governance regime built around them. Paul Kanjorski, Chairman of a US Congressional Committee, claimed after the Madoff fraud was exposed that the US regulatory system had failed and had to be completely rebuilt. But red flags had been waved. Independent commentators over the years raised suspicions about Madoff's business, and the SEC itself reviewed Madoff's businesses eight times in sixteen years and interviewed Madoff himself twice but found nothing.[52]

The inquiry into the collapse of Sir Allen Stanford's businesses, just starting at the time of writing, is also shedding light on the role of regulators and their enforcement regimes. Stanford's businesses had attracted attention from the regulators for years before they collapsed, accompanied by the usual crowd of red faces and forest of finger pointing. The Financial Industry Regulatory Authority (FINRA), the SEC's first line of defence when overseeing broker-dealers in the US, regularly conducted inspections of Stanford Group Company. They even issued fines of about $70,000 from April 2007, including one relating to Stanford's failure to provide 'fair and balanced' treatment of the risks and potential benefits of some of the investments. Financial analyst Alex Dalmady said that it took him just 20 minutes to create the spreadsheet that formed the basis of his analysis that led him to claim the company was a fraud.[53] But it was the collapse that stopped the business, not the regulators, despite their visits and fines.

A key element of the regulatory regime for incorporated entities in particular in most parts of the world is audit. The effect of any regulatory regime will be weakened if that regime is unable to provide some form of independent confirmation of compliance. Companies have their own rules and regulations, and reviewing compliance with these is the role of an internal audit department. 'Internal audit' might seem to some an oxymoron: how can an audit function have any independence if its staff have been recruited by, are paid by, and report to members of management? The effectiveness of internal audit depends therefore on the extent to which these concerns can be mitigated.

Common sense

A command by regulation approach to governance encourages behaviour contrary to common sense. The United States, a country where lawyers are unusually numerous and influential, throws up plenty of examples of what happens when rules are granted too much of the upper hand. In 2005 an American sued his dry cleaners for allegedly losing his trousers. He particularly took issue with the sign outside the shop which claimed, unfortunately so for the management, 'Satisfaction Guaranteed'. The plaintiff took the view that he was far from satisfied, and calculated his loss – after initially starting with $1,500 as a reasonable fine for consumer fraud, then multiplying it by 12 for the number of his complaints, and by 1,200 for the number of days he was deprived of his trousers, and by 3 for the number of owners in the shop, and adding still more for the inevitable and difficult to argue against 'mental anguish suffered' – at some $54 million. Though the case was dismissed, the dry cleaners found themselves landed with a legal bill of $100,000. That the plaintiff in question was a judge only serves to reinforce the perception in the minds of many that lawyers are as much the root of the problem as they are the route to a solution.[54] The case, which has gained a certain notoriety even in America, is discussed in legal reform campaigner Philip Howard's book *Life Without Lawyers*, a sustained argument that the law in America at least, where a woman has been allowed to sue McDonald's for serving her the coffee with which she scalded herself, and teachers can hardly maintain discipline for fear of being sued for maltreating the pupils left in their charge, has got out of hand. These scenarios are illustrative of an environment in which rule and regulation, instead of supporting the real world, have replaced it. It is a nightmare that governance regulators need to remember.

Notwithstanding these objections to governance by rule, the softer 'comply or explain' approach has been questioned. When the Financial Reporting Council (FRC) reviewed the Combined Code in 2007, the approach was described as working 'reasonably well' – hardly a ringing endorsement. In March 2009, and after another set of governance failures, the FRC reported: 'The effectiveness of the Combined Code and the "comply or explain" mechanism are being tested to a greater extent than under the previous, relatively benign conditions.'[55] At the time of writing the 'comply or explain' principle is under review again.

Perspectives on guidance versus prescription

In recent years management thinking has thrown up some interesting ideas on the functioning of rules in management systems – ideas that attempt to provide an appropriate context for rules. Shona Brown and Kathleen Eisenhardt in their book *Competing on the Edge*[56] draw instructive parallels with jazz. We all know that jazz is improvised, but we often forget the fact that at the heart of every improvisation is a firm set of rules. The whole team will agree on the melody before they start. Each player will take it in turn to embroider the melody and will stick to his allotted number of bars before handing the baton over. Much of jazz is indeed left to individual inspiration, but the rules are there all the same. The rules are few in number, but they cannot be broken. There are lessons in this parallel for governance frameworks. Identify and implement the rules and the policy needed to keep the system as a whole alive, but keep the rules to an absolute minimum, and police them rigorously. Where possible leave it to individual circumstance and ingenuity to develop practice that works. Turn the attention of the ingenious towards making the system work for them, and away from finding clever ways of avoiding it altogether.

Another interesting line of thinking is set out by Harvard Business School professor Robert Simons.[57] He points out the difference between negative rules and positive rules. Rules that tell you what you cannot do allow, by implication, considerable room for independent thinking to those who have to comply. You cannot wander into territory prohibited by the rules – but you can do everything else. On the other hand, rules that tell you what you *should do* are by definition a lot more constraining and allow a lot less room for manoeuvre.

As Simons points out, many of the best rule systems are principally negative. Nine out of the Ten Commandments are negative. A legal system based on case law (such as the British and American systems) rather than a prescriptive code (such as many European systems) also falls essentially into this category in that it tends to define what is prohibited rather than what is allowed. I'm sure it is not coincidental that the commercial environments in the US and the UK are more favourable to entrepreneurship than those in Continental Europe. As with the jazz approach to rules, this focus on the negative is another way of keeping rules to the minimum, allowing room for creativity and enterprise in the boardroom and around the management table. As Einstein observed, keep things as simple as possible, but no simpler.

The approach to the introduction of flexible hours demonstrated by a client I once worked with is instructive:

> When introducing flexible hours for staff my first
> reaction was to worry about a customer ringing up with
> no one around to answer the call, so I drafted rules and
> regulations to govern when staff could and could not
> flex their hours and how to record them. I ended up
> with a document that was horribly unwieldy, and that
> shouted 'I do not trust my staff'. So I scrapped it and
> turned to trust instead. Now staff know they have to
> work 37 hours in an ordinary week. How they get there,
> and how they organise cover, I leave to them. The system
> works well – and has the added advantage of improving
> communication in the office.

The example reminds us of another implication of rules. Rules that demand obeying imply organisations and the people responsible for them cannot be trusted to act in the best interests of their organisations or the stakeholders with an interest in them. But notwithstanding the precepts of agency theory, trust is an important concept in any management system, and particularly in a governance system that otherwise risks interfering in the internal workings of someone else's organisation. Trust is also something we will need to come back to.

To recap, the approach of the Combined Code reflects a preference for guidance over rules. It prefers general principles to detailed prescription. Rather than invest in an expensive enforcement regime, the Combined Code presumes a 'comply or explain' approach, trusting to transparency and communication rather than inspector and punishment. Such an approach invites controversy. In practice it is difficult to reconcile 'comply or explain' and guidance. As some of the stories told above demonstrate, a business that chooses to explain rather than comply often invites howls of derision from outsiders – a reaction consistent with breaking rules when in fact no rules have been broken. But the approach remains sound and yet flexible, and for one particularly good reason. A framework that is constructed on rules and regulations puts the onus on the regulator: a framework based on guidance and recommendation puts the onus on the regulated. In the final analysis it is the regulated that matter, not the regulators.

Rules for social enterprises

The Combined Code is not the only code in the governance arena, not even in the UK. Sectors of the economy that are of particular interest to the public, or that are potentially prone to abuse, are likely to be subject to governance-related rules and frameworks. The social enterprise sector, for example, which in addition to providing opportunities for doing good also potentially provides opportunities for the unscrupulous to line their own pockets at the expense of the gullible and

the government, has been the subject of governance attention. *Good Governance: A Code for the Voluntary and Community
Sector* (the 'VCS Code') was published in 2005 by the National
Governance Hub, a partnership of organisations working to
improve governance in charities and other voluntary and
community organisations. The development of the code was
the work of the Charity Commission in partnership with
the National Council for Voluntary Organisations (NCVO),
the Association of Chief Executives of Voluntary Organisations (ACEVO), Charity Trustee Networks and the Institute
of Chartered Secretaries and Administrators (ICSA). The VCS
Code was heralded as 'a practical and easy-to-use guide to
help charities develop good practice'. The Charity Commission noted that they 'fully endorse it, and would encourage
all charities – from large to small – to use it'.

A particular problem for social enterprises and charities
is that the dominant role within such organisations is played
by volunteers. Volunteers can sometimes afford to be cavalier
with rules, and a social enterprise that depends on volunteers
will sometimes have a tough time corralling them within any
internal management framework or rule system. External
code makers can have difficulty therefore where charities are
concerned.

The VCS Code is based on seven key principles that the
authors say have been designed to apply to any charity:

● board leadership

● the board in control

● the high-performance board

● board review and renewal

● board delegation

● board and trustee integrity

● board openness.

As is evident, the code focuses in particular on the role of the board of trustees, mirroring the focus of the Combined Code on the board of directors in a company. But useful attention is given to the role of the chief executive as the bridge between the (volunteer) trustees and the (salaried) management team.

Notwithstanding the problems inherent in codifying conduct in the social enterprise sector, there are codes that pay specific attention to particular corners, reflecting the diversity of the sector as a whole. Housing associations have had a code prepared for them by the National Housing Federation, accompanied by a book (*Governance … the Small Print: A Range of Model Governance Documents Covering Key Policy Areas,* currently in its second edition). Cooperatives have their own *Corporate Governance Code of Best Practice.* And, of course, many areas of the social enterprise sector have their own regulators and rule makers. When codes and rules can take account of the particular needs of a particular sub-sector they are more likely to have a specificity which will foster influence and authority.

The VCS Code, although its focus is on the particular needs of a specific sector, pays homage to the Combined Code, not least in its 'comply or explain' approach. However, without the punch provided by stock exchange officials, the charity sector's approach to 'comply or explain' is even further away from a rule-based approach than the Combined Code. 'This Code is not mandatory, and sets out best practice,' the VCS Code says: 'Organisations that comply with the Code are *invited* [my italics] to state this in their annual report and other relevant published material … Where an organisation does not comply with a specific part of the Code, it is *invited* also to record this fact, and to set out the reasons for non-compliance.'[58] Not only are charities invited to comply or explain, it is only by way of a gentlemanly invitation that they are expected to participate in the first place. The names of organisations that do comply are published, but nonetheless there is considerable freedom granted to those who choose not to comply, for bad reasons as well as good.

Codes with as few teeth as this are hardly rules at all, which to some, particularly those who believe that rules are made for breaking, begs the question as to whether such a code serves any meaningful purpose, or indeed whether corporate governance itself makes any sense without rules that can be applied and policed. The reality is that corporate governance fills in the space that the legislators have left blank – left blank usually for good reasons. In truth, of course, aspects of the social enterprise sector are very tightly regulated, leaving little room for governance codes to operate. Charities are one type of social enterprise sector that is tightly regulated, and charities benefit from some tax breaks in return. Most charities have to be registered with the Charity Commission, which also acts as regulator, and the few charities that are currently not obliged to register (some of the older educational institutions, museums, religious charities and some other organisations subject to their own regimes) are in effect subject to regulatory frameworks no less onerous than that managed by the Charity Commission for registered charities. Even these charities are now slowly being brought under the wing of the Charities Commission, following the Charities Act 2006.

Charities' objectives have always been tightly restricted. If anything the restrictions have been getting tighter in recent years. The 'public benefit' test has been a challenge for charities for a long time and is one of the key influences on the definition of a charity, but a new approach to interpreting 'public benefit' was introduced in the Charities Act 2006, and presents perhaps the biggest shake-up for charities in centuries. No longer are charities allowed to presume they benefit the public, but are required to demonstrate that they do, otherwise they will risk losing their charitable status (and the tax benefits that accompany). The government has left it to the Charity Commission to define what is meant by 'public benefit', thus providing enough material for debate and regulation to last a few centuries more. The Charity Commission's guidance notes, issued in January 2008, run to almost 20,000 words. Of particular controversy has been the application of the new public benefit test to private schools and hospitals, which have benefited from charitable status from time immemorial, but now have problems. Schools charging fees, for example, are required to 'think about other ways that people who cannot afford those fees can benefit'. Charities' ability to conduct commercial business is also severely restricted, as is their ability to pay their key officials. With such a tight regulatory framework it is perhaps inevitable that a governance code is always going to be relatively incidental.

However, even in charities, a totally rule-based approach is never going to work all the time. The gap has to be filled by codes. Undoubtedly this leaves principle, guidance and comply or explain approaches to governance exposed to the wiles of those so-minded, individuals who have the same approach to governance that they do to tax: if there is a loophole, exploit it; if there is not a loophole it is because you and your advisers are not working hard enough to find it; if the rule makers are weak enough to set guidelines rather than rules, interpret this as an invitation to ignore them. Recent history has shown that such individuals can be put under pressure by exposure, but rule and punishment is not the only way of leveraging influence. In addition to codes, transparency and publicity can help. Making sure organisations have the right people in the right places is most important of all. Once again, bad governance relies on rules: good governance is about roles.

A final note on 'comply or explain' and codes. In June 2008 the FSA's new Corporate Governance Rules implementing EU requirements with respect to audit committees and governance statements took effect. Listed companies are now obliged by regulation to include a statement on corporate governance in their directors' reports. Such a statement must include a reference to which governance regimen, compulsory or voluntary, the company is subject to; and which practices the company is following that are beyond the requirements of national law. The company is also now obliged to 'comply or explain' as a matter of regulation. Presumably they are not required to comply or explain whether or not they have chosen to comply or explain.

Family business governance

Perhaps even more interesting than the codes adopted operating in the not-for-profit sectors is the codification of governance adopted by many of the world's largest and most sophisticated family businesses. A large family business that has been in family ownership for many generations will often have a very complicated shareholder base, with shareholders from different branches of the family and different generations. Many will have non-family shareholders as well. But unless they have chosen to list their shares on a stock exchange, most family businesses find themselves outside the scope of the governance regulations.

Governance, however, or the lack thereof, is often at the heart of many family business problems, triggered by suspicion and lack of trust between different family members, who may or may not be involved in the business as managers, employees or shareholders. Sophisticated family businesses will invest time in structuring relationships that might otherwise be left to chance. The family's conclusions about the relationship they want to have with their business and each other are often formally written down and recorded in a document. Families use different labels for this documentation, with some describing it as their 'family constitution' and others talking about their 'creed' or 'charter'. Smaller businesses with simpler needs might refer just to a memorandum of understanding or even a shareholders' agreement. But all families that take governance seriously take the trouble to commit their understanding of it to paper. In so doing they find themselves drafting their own, private, governance codes.

A constitution is essentially a statement of the family's shared values and policies in relation to ownership and the operation of the business. It represents a powerful tool in establishing and maintaining the balance between the best interests of the business on the one hand, and the well-being of the family on the other. It also fosters clarity and helps reduce the selective amnesia that all human beings suffer from: especially the ability of family members to forget discussions and decisions that do not suit their own perspective.

A family constitution often addresses the following key issues:

- the family's agreed long-term vision and its goals for the business

- the core elements of its family values and management philosophy

- equity ownership policies – the rights and responsibilities of owners

- the conditions under which family members enter and exit the business

- rules covering family jobs – remuneration, incentives, appraisal and reporting lines

- the relationship between family shareholders and the board

- the agreed criteria for management succession

- relationships within the family – covering, for instance, the responsibilities of family members towards each other, family meetings, how communication is to be encouraged and promoted, and how differences between family branches and other conflicts should be dealt with.

As well as the subjects listed above, some families use the opportunity to go further, making their constitution into a sort of vision statement that records the family's agreed stance, not just in relation to the business, but also on a range of moral, behavioural and philanthropic issues. Initially, discussion centres on seeking out common ground in relation to the business, but, once this level of consensus has been achieved, an appreciation often develops among family members that their ability to agree on business issues reflects the fact that, at a deeper level, they share a common set of ethical, moral and spiritual beliefs.

Family members generally hope that the finished document will be a confidential family statement of intent rather than an enforceable legal agreement. But, as detailed provisions start to come under the microscope, legal enforceability may be desirable.

A theme of this book is that all good governance is alive, not a fossilised, ceremonial structure that hangs around the business as a memory of what was once a useful discussion. For the family constitution to be regarded as a 'living' document, provision should be made for it to be reviewed every four or five years as the family and the business grows and develops. In the meantime, there should be mechanisms allowing family members to record any constitutional concerns or worries prior to the next formal review.

Family businesses, big and small, listed and unlisted, have taken governance seriously for a long time; indeed long before the establishment of regulatory authorities like the FSA or SEC. The Mogi family, behind Kikkoman soy sauce and related products, was founded in 1630. It has benefited from a family constitution since about 1800. Indeed, the most ambitious family businesses have long recognised that if they want the business to last and not be damaged by the inevitable stresses that the family will be subject to, it will need to take its governance seriously. Family businesses draft and adopt constitutions and other governance documents as a matter of choice. In so doing they send a message to the rest of the commercial community about the value of governance – and the role codes can play in facilitating it.

Partnership rules and codes

Professional partnerships are another type of organisation with an interesting relationship with the regulation and code makers. In some senses partnerships have had the luxury for a large part of their history of being able to exempt themselves from some of the most fundamental prescriptions of corporate governance. Historically partnerships have been secretive organisations, without even a requirement for an external audit, or even the need to publish financial statements. This has been a consequence of two characteristics of partnerships. Firstly, their owner-managed status has helped. Private businesses in many parts of the world are still under no obligation to have an audit, and often can keep their numbers close to their chests. In the UK private companies have had to file accounts and, above a size, to have had them audited. But many partnerships in the UK have been required to do neither. Secondly, as noted in Chapter 3, partners in traditional partnerships have had unlimited, joint and several liability for their actions. In addition to there being little or no divide between the owners and the managers, the owner-managers risk everything they have on the quality of their service. Partnerships' lack of ability to enjoy limited liability and their ability to be secretive about their affairs go hand in hand. It is in part because a limited liability company can limit the liability of its shareholders that it has been deemed necessary that they open their financial affairs to the public. Otherwise a supplier or lender might put themselves at the mercy of an unscrupulous shareholder able to hide behind 'the veil of incorporation'. For partnerships the converse has been true.

On the other hand, partnerships have often found themselves subject to rules and regulations that other types of organisation have escaped from. Professional service partnerships in particular have been subject to external regulation. More than one profession has *insisted* for example that its member firms organise themselves as partnerships. Professional supervisory bodies have also had occasion to regulate who is allowed to be a partner in a member firm. This has had the consequence in some industries of preventing 'mixed' service partnerships, when left to their own devices many professionals from different disciplines would have considered setting up in partnership together.

Well-managed partnerships, like well-managed family businesses, have chosen to define their own governance regulations. Partnerships govern their affairs using a partnership agreement – in effect a combination of a shareholders' agreement and a memorandum and articles of association for the partnership. Partnerships have considerable freedom when drafting these agreements (indeed, whether to draft one at all). But a well-drafted partnership agreement will contain, *inter alia*, the following typical clauses:

- The business of the firm – important because this will indicate the extent to which partners (ever mindful of their unlimited liability) authorise each other to bind the firm.

- The duration of the firm and the circumstances under which it might be dissolved. Without this clause a partnership will and can be dissolved by any one partner giving notice.

- Partnership property – thus defining what belongs to the firm and what is the personal property of individual partners.

- Partnership capital – how the firm is to be financed, the role third-party finance is to play, how partners are required to contribute capital and on what terms, and how capital arrangements are to be changed.

- How profits and losses, both capital and revenue, are to be calculated and allocated to individual partners, drawing mechanisms and benefits. Firms differ markedly in their profit-sharing mechanisms. Some will go for the simple approach and share profits equally, but simple does not necessarily mean effective. Other firms will choose to formalise a basis for sharing profits unequally, perhaps with reference to seniority or performance.

- Tax – partners are self-employed, but some firms will choose to retain tax and pay it on behalf of the partners; others will expect individual partners to settle their own tax affairs.

- Restrictions and duties – governing whether partners will be allowed to offer services personally; matters of exclusivity and confidentiality; restrictive covenants.

- Management and decision-taking processes – including many of the matters referred to earlier such as voting rights and delegated authorities.

- Partnership and management meetings.

- Promotion – mechanisms for admitting new individuals to the partnership.

- Outgoing partners – procedures governing the circumstances in which partners are to be allowed to retire, or circumstances in which the firm reserves the right to expel a partner.

- Mechanisms for resolving internal disputes.

- Mechanisms for changing the partnership agreement itself.

This list is neither complete nor comprehensive, but gives a good idea of the nature of a partnership agreement. Individuals planning to set up a partnership are well advised to take specialist legal advice before going too far.

As has already been noted, traditional partnerships have been voting with their feet to become limited liability partnerships (LLPs) in the UK, thus securing for the partners in the firm a significant measure of the protection previously only afforded to the shareholders in a limited company. In return for this, LLPs have been obliged to welcome in some of the key governance controls. LLPs, unlike traditional *unlimited* liability partnerships, have to publish financial statements, and these have to be audited too.

The legal framework that governs LLPs is different from that governing traditional partnerships, but for a group of lay people looking in, the governance arrangements are similar. Indeed, many are the partnerships that have converted to an LLP with the express intention of (as far as is possible) carrying on business as normal. The language changes: LLPs have 'members' not 'partners' and they therefore have members' agreements rather than partnership agreements, but the document can be expected to cover much the same territory. LLPs have 'designated members' too – members who are formally identified as being responsible for certain important administrative roles, including matters relating to accounts, filing and auditors.

This is just the start of a bigger trend seeing some professional partnerships becoming more subject to the sort of externally imposed governance frameworks that listed companies have long been accustomed to. Of special interest have been those partnerships operating in industries of particular public interest, in whose activities numbers of stakeholders might increasingly have an interest. A good example is the audit profession. A listed company will be audited by a partnership, and the shareholders of the company will have a significant interest, not just in the company, but in the quality and reliability of the audit firm's work. If it is in the shareholders' interests that the company be subject to externally determined standards of governance, why should it not also be in their interests that the auditors be subject to similar standards? At the time of writing, an independent Audit Firm Governance Working Group has been established by the Institute of Chartered Accountants of England and Wales to respond to an invitation from the Financial Reporting Council to support Recommendation 14 of the October 2007 report of the Market Participants' Group, which stated that: 'Every firm that audits public interest entities should comply with the provisions of a Combined Code-style best practice corporate governance guide or give a considered explanation.'

The project will be completed soon. In the meantime it is to be observed that the Combined Code was designed for a different set of circumstances from that presented by audit firms. The shareholders in a partnership, including an LLP, are the partners, and they stand in different relation to their firms than the shareholders in a listed company do to the directors of the listed company. Yes, the shareholders in the listed clients of an audit firm *do* have an interest in the governance of their auditors, but this stakeholder group stands at two further removes from the management of an audit firm when compared with their relation to the board of the company in which they own shares. Similarly, just as the Combined Code is not deemed necessary to safeguard the interests of private shareholders in a private company, so a code should not be necessary to safeguard the interests of partners in a partnership.

Yet the notion of a code for audit firms does have significant merit. Such a code might well recognise the interests of the shareholders of the clients of audit firms, though it will need to recognise that this presents potentially a fundamentally different issue for audit firms from that addressed by the Combined Code on behalf of listed companies. Partners in audit firms might be uncomfortable on occasion with the implications, but they would acknowledge that shareholders of the clients of audit firms are obviously keenly interested in the quality, robustness and independence of the audit process, and the extent to which the audit firm in question manages itself so as to deliver these, and that this is a key governance issue. The sustainability of an audit firm, for example, as far as the shareholders of the client of that audit firm is concerned, is entirely related to the quality of the firm's audit process, and only remotely related to the internal governance arrangements in the practice itself. Indeed, shareholders of clients of audit firms would not want a firm to be sustained, no matter how sophisticated its internal governance processes, if its audit processes were not satisfactory. Nevertheless, the robustness of the audit and the quality of the audit firm itself is also a matter of interest to external stakeholders and therefore it seems reasonable that audit firms of public interest entities should participate in some form of externally monitored governance framework, even if such a code for audit firms restricts itself to focusing on the extent to which the firm manages itself so as to deliver effective audits.

In reality some audit firms – indeed some partnerships from different professions – are already adopting a number of the standard governance prescriptions. BDO, chartered accountants (and auditors, of course), have already appointed two non-executive directors, not because they have to but because they see value in the appointments. I am sure that partnerships, particularly those intimately involved in business in which the public at large perceives itself as having a stake, will continue to explore and apply governance methodology for themselves, and will learn from the hard-won experience of listed companies as they do so.

7 Performance measurement and management

'Measure what is measurable, and make measurable what is not so.'

Galileo Galilei

Performance measurement and management mechanisms, and reward systems in particular, are cornerstones of every management system, and unsurprisingly are the focus of much thinking under the heading of corporate governance, and the subject of many rules, regulations and guidance notes in the governance codes. Mechanisms for remunerating the individuals who are responsible for the key decisions in a company receive considerable attention in the Combined Code. Performance management and measurement, and performance-based remuneration, are not just subjects of corporate governance, they are levers for delivering governance as well. Rules and regulations are imposed by external agencies, but for governance to have real impact and influence it needs to be internalised. Managers need to mean it, not just say it and write it. Performance management and measurement systems, though often the target of regulators, are at least designed by insiders for the benefit of insiders, and have a better chance of having influence.

There are two fundamental premises here: that measurement is a key, if not *the* key component of a control system, and that people respond to remuneration systems (if you pay them to do something they are more likely to do it than if their pay is actually determined by something else). The first premise is summed up in an often repeated maxim: 'If you cannot measure it you cannot manage it.' Switch this around and we have a recipe for perfect management: make sure you have the right measurement tools and you can manage anything. Hence the power wielded by statisticians and accountants, and the measures they provide for us. Key performance indicators, gross and net profit, return on capital employed; means, modes and medians; utilisation, productivity and asset turnover; variances and deviations (standard, and tailored at considerable expense to each organisation's peculiar circumstances) – all these give management reports credibility and managers the illusion of control. That the aura of authority and factuality that surrounds so many of these indicators is illusory explains why so much of performance measurement – indeed, the whole accounting profession – is subject to so much governance regulation and guidance. It also helps explain why in so many organisations the corporate governance agenda, whether it relates to accounts or not, is the responsibility of the finance department.

However, what is true of rules (discussed above) – that they struggle to capture the detail of reality in a meaningful and manageable way – is also true of management and measurement systems. The more we wrestle with our businesses, the more we seek to perfect the dashboards and the indicators that tell us how our businesses are performing, and the more we try and deduce actionable conclusions from them, the more it becomes evident that much of what really matters within the business continues to escape our attention, notwithstanding (or perhaps because of) the increasingly sophisticated measurement methodologies at our disposal. Businesses are always far too complicated to be reduced to the easily measurable (as well as the easily enforceable). Indeed, it is almost as if what really matters cannot be measured at all. This is because businesses at heart are about people, and people refuse to respond logically to management stimuli in the way they are supposed to, or to be tidied up by key performance indicators. It would be unfortunate to have to conclude that, if a business cannot be properly measured, it cannot be properly managed either.

There are many instances of managers seeking unreal comforts in the easily measurable and coming, as a consequence, to unfortunate ends. One particularly meaningful illustration of the consequences of an over-concern with what can be easily measured has come to be called McNamara's fallacy, after Robert McNamara, US Secretary of Defense at the time of the Vietnam War, who was reduced to measuring military success in terms of the ratio of Viet Cong casualties to US casualties. Logical reductionism of this type has led decision takers down all sorts of management blind alleys (and worse, in the case of McNamara). As Charles Handy has observed, the first step down the alley is to measure whatever can be easily measured. This is OK as far as it goes. The second step is to disregard what cannot be easily measured or to give it an arbitrary quantitative value. This is artificial and misleading. The third step is to presume that what cannot be measured is not really important. This is blindness. The fourth step is to say what cannot be measured does not exist. This is suicide.[59]

That measurement misses aspects of a business's performance that are critical, or can foster distorted behaviour on the part of even well-meaning people, is well known. Not that the knowledge stops managers from inventing and reinventing mechanisms for measuring performance. In October 2006 the Healthcare Commission reported that there were serious and significant failings in the way bosses at Stoke Mandeville Hospital in Aylesbury, Buckinghamshire had dealt with two *Clostridium difficile* infections. It noted that lessons had not been not learned from the first outbreak of the bug at the hospital between October 2003 and June 2004. When a second outbreak had struck in 2005, senior managers did not bring it quickly under control because they prioritised other objectives, such as the government's targets on Accident and Emergency waiting times, the Commission reported. Managers' determination to meet the government's target for a maximum waiting time in A&E of four hours led to some patients with diarrhoea being kept in or put on open wards rather than in isolation facilities.[60] It is easy in retrospect to suspect the existence of and therefore to look for stupidity, even villainy. But at heart the Stoke Mandeville story is about governance. Bright people will do stupid things if they are encouraged to do them by clumsy management and measurement systems. What most managers and commentators fail to realise is that most management and measurement systems are clumsy – indeed they *have to be* clumsy if they are to have any chance of influencing behaviour.

One of the most common, and increasingly controversial, manifestations of a connection between measurement and management is performance-related remuneration. Every performance-based remuneration system has a measurement mechanism at heart. Unfortunately, the mechanics of connecting pay to performance are difficult to establish effectively. If you want individuals to be *influenced* by their remuneration then you have to avoid making their incentive packages too complicated. Too many variables and most human beings will throw their hands in the air and carry on doing what they would have done had they not been given performance-related pay in the first place. (Again, it is the same with laws and rules.) Then the only people to benefit from the scheme will be the consultants paid for setting it up. The fact is that most senior team members' roles *are* complicated, and the individuals that hold them are responsible for dozens of variables, many of which sit uncomfortably with each other, if not conflict. To connect remuneration to all aspects of such an individual's performance is an impossible task. To connect remuneration to just a selection of 'the most important' of an individual's deliverables is to invite dysfunctional behaviour as staff will be encouraged to focus on those aspects of their roles that will increase their incomes at the expense of those that do not.

For any senior role, therefore, it can be difficult coming up with individually tailored performance targets. For the really top guys, rather than look for personal targets the sensible thing for many is to look for corporate targets. If the business does well then the individual will do well. This takes us right into the heart of corporate governance of course: if what you really want is to align the interests of directors and the interests of the businesses they lead, make sure directors are rewarded when these businesses do well. But determining when a business does well can in itself be difficult. Determining profit is an art, not a matter of fact. And seemingly healthy profits one year might be bought at the cost of the long-term health of the company. There is many a senior banker whose million-dollar bonuses in 2005 and 2006 looked much less justifiable when the credit crunch crunched and when the earnings on which they were based turned out to be less than factual. Besides, paying somebody when a business does well is easy; not paying the same individual when the business does poorly is much more difficult. Pay is always easier to give than to take away. Bankers – those that survived – were still receiving bonuses in 2009.

Equity in the remuneration package

The tidiest way of connecting a director's remuneration to the interests of the business or the interests of shareholders is to give her shares, and to require her to hold them for an extended period of time. Cash is inherently short-term, while equity surely rewards the long-term performance that shareholders seek. 'Equity should be used to foster or reward commitment,' argues entrepreneur, venture capitalist and London Business School professor John Bates.[61] If you are looking to recruit or reward knowledge, or experience, you should be prepared to pay for it when you use it – with cash. Many businesses are not this discriminating. Equity is now an expected component of the package of a senior member of any business, big or small, public or private. But equity as remuneration is better in theory than it is in practice. Directors can do very well, but in a bear market the value of shares will go down anyway. Conversely, many a fool has been rewarded for being lucky enough to ride off the back of a bull market. It is also a little presumptuous to assume that equity-based remuneration will align directors and shareholders anyway. The problem is not necessarily the directors. Pinning down the motives of the ultimate shareholders in a listed company, in which blocks of shares are controlled by institutions on behalf of individuals, is difficult; and even if you assume that all such shareholders want is a decent return, then this in itself is difficult to reconcile with the real decisions that directors have to take every day, laden with uncertainty, risk and the pressures of entrepreneurship.

Giving and receiving shares in a private company has its own complications. Being given a slice of the equity of an unlisted company is not the same as being given equity in a business whose shares have a ready market. To be given equity inevitably begs questions about when those shares might be sold and in what circumstances. A new member of the management team with equity is thus likely to have at the very least half an eye on a financial strategy that will enable him to realise his investment – which might have very little to do with the interests, long- or short-term, of the other shareholders. In my experience it is common for newcomers to a management team to be surprised to find that existing owner-managers have not given any serious thought to 'exit'. Hopefully, therefore, equity or equity-based remuneration should force a discussion about the alignment of personal and corporate objectives, but it may not guarantee the alignment in itself. Indeed, it may provoke the opposite. As one observer claims, 'If you want managers to act in their shareholders' interests, take away their company stock'.[62] Perhaps less extreme is the perception that many owner-managers just use equity-based remuneration as a strategy for not paying market salaries in the first place. Similarly, I remember well the HR director who told me her firm had decided to scrap bonus schemes because a bonus was just an excuse for not paying someone properly to start off with.

In recent years, executives have received options over equity as an important component of their remuneration packages. For many businesses thinking about equity as an incentive, share options can look like another way of having your cake and eating it. Assuming options are granted at least at current business value, an option will only become a share if the business increases in value. It is easy to be cynical about options. Dot.coms in the dot.com boom years shed share options like confetti, which did little to improve their credibility. Option schemes are inherently complicated and expensive to establish. Also, because the individual probably will not have to give much if anything for them at the outset, it is easy to see option schemes as all gain and no pain, and therefore not nearly so great a motivation as might at first appear. Additionally, as with equity, options are only mean-ingful if the holder can at least imagine a time when they are realisable. On the other hand, even if you do not think they are a good idea, the chancellor of the exchequer often does, and there are some tax-efficient options mechanisms around, particularly for the smaller, private business. All shareholders and potential shareholders are to be advised, however, not to let tax complicate the picture. Tax is the cart not the horse. Work out what you want to achieve, then work out the most tax-effective way of delivering it.

But the real truth about options is that neither companies giving them, nor shareholders receiving them, have really thought of them as aligning the interests of shareholders and management. When options sink 'under water' – that is, the price of the shares subject to the option decline in value to a position where it would be cheaper to buy the shares on the market rather than via the option – some companies have been only too quick to reprice the options using the lower share price as a reference point, arguing that managers still need an 'incentive' even though their performance to date has only resulted in the share price declining. Cynicism of this sort on the part of managers demonstrates that, for many, an option is really a deferred performance-related bonus masquerading as a mechanism for aligning managers with shareholders. As with most fudges it often achieves neither objective. If a man-ager's performance does not warrant a bonus, the manager should not receive a bonus and *should* be disappointed. To give out bonuses when performance is poor is 'shameful', as Barack Obama has put it. That a company believes it needs to give bonuses despite poor performance suggests either base pay is wrong and options are being used as an excuse for not paying properly to start off with, or that remuneration is connected to the wrong measure of performance, or that the reward has nothing to do with performance in the first place.

If you think you're aligning your managers with shareholders when you award options you are living in a fool's paradise. Option holders get far more upside than downside compared to shareholders. Repricing options to ensure managers get something anyway only focuses attention on this difference, and rubs shareholders' noses in it. Repricing options has the effect therefore of alienating managers from shareholders, not aligning them.

Much of the governance fuss about remuneration has been generated not so much by the nature of the remuneration given to directors as by the amount. It is only too easy to pick examples, there being so many. Let's take one of the more obvious – Dick Fuld, erstwhile CEO of Lehman Brothers. House of Representatives Oversight Committee Chairman Henry Waxman reeled off details of Mr Fuld's large art collection, several houses and what he said was the 'half a billion dollars' that the chief executive had taken home over his time at the helm of the company, and then asked Fuld to compare all this with the losses faced by shareholders and the damage done to the wider economy. 'Is that fair?' Mr Waxman asked. Mr Fuld answered: 'The majority of my compensation came in stock. The vast majority of stock I got I still owned at the point of our filing ... The $500 million number is not accurate, although it is still a large number.'[63] Even so, how many tens or hundreds of millions are needed to align a director with his company or his company's shareholders? When does a bonus or a handout of shares or stock or options cease being an incentive and start just being a reflection of greed on the part of the directors, and an indication of the power of the board and its committees to deliver to its members enough wealth to safeguard the interests of a director and his family for generations to come, regardless as to whether or not the interests of shareholders or any other stakeholders have been served? When an individual is earning as much from a listed business as Fuld was from Lehman Brothers, even if a large part of the remuneration is in the form of shares, it is misleading to suggest that his interests were being aligned with those of his shareholders. Fuld's remuneration was at the expense of his shareholders – and that was even before the bank he led went bust.

Other perspectives

When temperatures get very hot the laws of physics as mere mortals understand them start breaking down. When the numbers are investment-bank-big or the incentive to focus on one objective to the exclusion of all others is extreme, individuals start behaving strangely, even inhumanly. As the story about Robert McNamara and Vietnam illustrates, talk of suicide and death is not overly dramatic. In other contexts linkages between performance, measurement, incentive and reward lead capable and otherwise well-meaning individuals to behave dangerously, both as far as others and themselves are concerned. Sports events of all kinds are perpetually conducted under the grisly shadow of drugs and drug testing. Merely prohibiting drug-enhanced performance is not sufficient – it seems the glory that comes with success is a more powerful motivator than the threat of being caught breaking a rule of the sport or even the law of the land (corporate governance code makers take note). Not even the threat of serious self-harm or premature death is a sufficient deterrent – the number of early obituaries for erstwhile world-record-holding athletes with suspicious musculatures is growing. More sophisticated detection devices and better-equipped laboratories merely have the consequence of increasing the cunning of the drugs scientists interested in sustaining their clients' chances of winning. The *Guardian* newspaper is not unusual in wondering whether the Tour de France will ever be able to recover some sense of integrity. Maybe cycling as a sport is just doomed. Essentially the problem is presented as one of incentives – a key area of governance. 'It will do so only if much more effective action is taken on three vital levels: the testing, the punishment and the indoctrination of the riders ... Signing pledges is no longer enough.' Changing the riders' mentality would appear to be the most intractable problem, and inherently related to the rewards. One interesting if partial solution was proposed by Marc Coucke, Chairman of the pharmaceutical company that was the main sponsor of the Predictor-Lotto team. Confronting the claim that prize money is the true motive for doping, he announced that he would pay his riders according to their attitude rather than their results.[64]

What Coucke is in effect attempting to do is to decouple rewards from the objectives of the sport – winning – doing precisely the opposite from what is recommended by most regular corporate governance thinking, which is ensuring through remuneration that managers and directors are focused on results. The Combined Code again:

> Levels of remuneration should be sufficient to attract,
> retain and motivate directors of the quality required
> to run the company successfully, but a company
> should avoid paying more than is necessary for this
> purpose. A significant proportion of executive directors'
> remuneration should be structured so as to link rewards
> to corporate and individual performance.

Every element of this prescription is an element in a very tall order, however. Bearing in mind the extremes cited already in this chapter, what does 'sufficient' mean? At what level is a company paying 'more than is necessary'? What is a 'significant proportion'? And does linking performance to reward work anyway? Alfie Kohn in his book *Punished by*

Rewards[65] argues that performance-based reward ultimately acts as a disincentive. The concept operates alright in the short term, but in the long term performance-based reward just does not work. Kohn even argues that performance-based reward discourages risk taking: individuals will do what they need to do to get the reward, and then no more. Quality champion W. E. Deming is more fulsome: '... [the system by which merit is appraised and rewarded is] ... the most powerful inhibitor to quality and productivity in the Western world ... [It] nourishes short-term performance, annihilates long-term planning, builds fear, demolishes teamwork, nourishes rivalry and ... leaves people bitter.'[66]

Unfortunately for Kohn's thesis, people do have to get paid something, and his book is much weaker when making recommendations for remuneration strategies that do not punish. Remuneration continues, therefore, to be an intractable problem for those responsible for governance frameworks inside and outside organisations. Such individuals stand a better chance of putting remuneration in its place if they at least appreciate the complex nature of the problem they are dealing with; if they recognise and protect their companies and their stakeholders from the consequences of an over-powerful director and the influence she might have, directly or indirectly, on her own remuneration; if they recognise how reward for achievement is different from incentive for performance not yet delivered; if they appreciate how, at an indeterminable level that differs from individual to individual, incentive turns into greed, which is something quite different and in nobody's interests, not even the director.

Establishing the right remuneration levels in a small business brings challenges all of its own. The first finance director in a business, the recruitment of whom marks a key stage in the evolution of governance in a growing business, can seem particularly expensive. He is quite likely to be the highest-paid employee in a young business – but as one venture capitalist puts it: 'I always tell companies we're looking to invest in, that a quality finance director will more than pay for himself within a year.' 'A good finance director is a business angel who brings something worth much more than money,' observes one successful entrepreneur. 'The finance director is usually under-rewarded compared to the CEO (who is usually over-rewarded …!)' argues another venture capitalist. It is not just the fact that accountants are expensive that accounts for the differential. A founding entrepreneur is inevitably motivated by more than money. That explains why many entrepreneurs give up well-paid jobs to put their businesses together. But any senior manager recruited to a business that is already established has motivations that are inherently different from those of the founder. Money will almost inevitably mean more. Many businesses without a decent finance director will still argue they cannot afford one and will leave the recruitment of an FD until too late, and the control of the most important governance element in the business to someone who is unqualified and unable to add serious value.

Unsurprisingly, many founders of new businesses look for ways of structuring a remuneration package that allows the business to keep the cake whilst giving the candidate the illusion of enjoying eating it. Giving directors options, or equity, is often seen as a route to making them very rich if they happen to work for major listed companies. In smaller businesses, as noted before, it is more likely to be an excuse for not paying them properly in the first place.

Other weapons in the performance management armoury

It can be easily forgotten in all this talk of rewarding people to do well and taking their rewards away (or not) if they perform badly, that performance management is not just a matter of remuneration. Performance management is about appraisal and assessment, and then training and development. Individuals, even key individuals, will not just do the right thing if the money is right. Appraisal, assessment, training and development should be key components of any governance framework, as should forms of non-financial recognition such as title, promotion, status and authority.

The Combined Code gives attention to the appraisal and assessment of the board. 'The board should undertake a formal and rigorous annual evaluation of its own performance and that of its committees and individual directors.'[67] The chairman is enjoined to act on the results of the performance evaluation exercise 'by recognising the strengths and addressing the weaknesses of the board and, where appropriate, proposing new members be appointed to the board or seeking the resignation of directors'.[68] How the board is reviewed is required to be disclosed in the annual report. In addition, the Combined Code requires that directors put themselves up for re-election at regular intervals of no more than three years, subject to satisfactory performance. Non-executive directors who serve for longer than nine years (three three-year terms) are required to be re-elected annually.

Sir Andrew Likierman, now Dean of London Business School, writing in an Institute of Chartered Accountants publication,[69] notes that the Combined Code's focus on 'performance' is somewhat less ambitious than 'success'. Likierman also notes that, though the Code suggests otherwise, most of its prescriptions and recommendations for appraisal focus on individuals and not the board as a whole. The observation is astute. Much governance is aimed at ensuring that one individual is not allowed to commit the sort of sins that individuals, no matter how brilliant, are inclined to commit if given too much power. Many of the checks and balances that are a consequence of governance thinking are based on a premise that collective thinking is likely to be more powerful, astute and prescient than thinking generated by an individual in isolation. The most important team in any company is the board. Likierman proposes ten key measures for assessing the success of the board:

- The starting point
    1   Ability to choose the right members
    2   Agreement about priorities in its role
    3   Agreement about how to achieve company strategy

- Process and relationships
    4   Effective in dispatching business in and between meetings
    5   Good internal board dynamics
    6   Good key relationships

- Coverage
    7   Focuses on key issues and risks
    8   Initiative-taking, dealing with crises and identifying emerging issues

- Impact
    9   Contributes to the company's performance

- Sustainability
    10   Aware of and interested in good practice

Likierman proposes asking individual directors to

comment on the success of the board using these ten criteria, and then requiring the chairman to facilitate a board discussion using the data collected in aggregate.

Likierman notes that the Combined Code is intended for listed companies, but claims that his approach will be of value to unlisted companies seeking long-term shareholder value, and also public sector organisations as well. I agree – and advise charities and not-for-profits and the management teams of partnerships to follow his recommendations as well.

Interestingly – perhaps revealingly – the Combined Code gives little attention to training. The word does not appear in the document, though the company secretary, as delegated by the chairman, is assigned the task of 'facilitating induction and assisting with professional development as required,'[70] and non-executives are encouraged in addition to 'regularly update and refresh their skills, knowledge and familiarity with the company'.[71] Many directors of companies do indeed consider themselves to be above personal development, or consider that training is something to be promoted out of almost an admission of inadequacy. At the same time, at the heart of many corporate governance failures are boards of directors without the skills, knowledge or experience either to provide a robust challenge to the executive, or to participate fully in key, complex, expensive decisions. Of course it is possible to argue that no one should be appointed to a board without the appropriate skills and knowledge. For many businesses this is a truth more honoured in the breach than the observance. Certainly there is no reason why an individual promoted from within a business to the board should fully appreciate the nature of the new role. When appointing an individual from outside, even an individual with board experience, it is surely less than wise to assume appropriate knowledge. A good interview will help, but can only go so far. Boards of trustees of charities in particular, comprised as they are of volunteers, are often woefully ignorant of the nature of their roles, the extent of their legal liabilities, and their relation as non-executives to the salaried, executive members of the organisation. But I have run many courses for directors on their directors' duties and responsibilities, and have given up being amazed how little many individuals know. Of course, if the individuals fully appreciated their responsibilities then they would not be on the course in the first place. Some board members come along together. Indeed, developing Sir Andrew Likierman's thinking a little further, there is some training and development activity that boards would benefit from undertaking together.

Appraisal, training and development are not just matters for the appointments committee. In a rapidly changing world they are live issues. The costs of not taking them seriously far outweigh the time and financial costs required to invest in them properly. Professional institutes and organisations acknowledge this and oblige their members to comply with continuing professional development. There is no recognised qualification for board directors, certainly not one that means that the personal development of directors even of listed companies can be taken for granted. There have been calls to make a profession of management in the same way as accountancy and law.[72] In my view there are considerable obstacles to making this a reality. In the meantime, Lord Myners's views on the typical bank board in 2008 deserve repeating: 'a retirement home for the great and the good'. As a politician his remarks have perhaps been heightened for rhetorical effect, but they hardly lend support to a view that board members of even the most sophisticated businesses are beyond training and development.

The ultimate weapon in the performance management armoury is dismissal. Directors of companies do indeed lose their jobs when the business does badly. The average tenure of a CEO seems to be shortening all the time. But directors when they fall tend to 'fall upwards', and many who fail in one senior role seem to pop up on the board of another company. Or if they fall downwards, their fall is cushioned by a termination payment that makes, no doubt, the experience for many seem very worthwhile.

All in all, performance management, certainly as far as directors are concerned, is an area of governance that has room to evolve further.

8 | Values and culture

'Leaders must encourage their organizations to
dance to forms of music yet to be heard.'

Warren Bennis[73]

Incentive schemes are hard, no-nonsense levers of organisational control, and they are comfortingly, even if mislead-
ingly, black and white. They can be subjected to scrutiny by
external agencies and regulators. It is no surprise therefore
that incentives take up so much time and attention when
managers are thinking about governance in their own organisations. It is also no surprise that they tend to be unpopular.
Also, as we have seen already, incentive mechanisms, and
rules for that matter, do not go nearly far enough to control
or influence the modern organisation in all its complexity.

When managers attempt to manage and control the parts
of the business that are beyond the realm of measurement
and remuneration they start exploring such matters as an
organisation's values, and its culture. These are also internally
generated rather than externally imposed, but because they
are softer and more difficult to define they are also impossible to regulate. An organisation's values show themselves
in all sorts of ways – including the complicated tangle of
custom, anecdote and unwritten codes of conduct that influence how and why things really get done. Make no mistake,

an organisation's culture and values set are hugely influential components in its governance system, the more so because in many organisations culture and values, though internally generated are often accidentally generated, and go not just uncodified but even unrecognised. Indeed, much as there are some cultures in the world (usually described as 'primitive') who still believe that a handshake and a verbal agreement are far more binding than a written contract, so there are attitudes and traits in some organisations that are so prevalent that they do not need writing down. Rules are made to be broken; values are not made in the first place, they just are.

Definition difficulties

The larger and more complicated the business, the harder it is to define values. At heart values are things held dear by individuals. So values become less distinctive and thus less influential when an organisation has to satisfy the different needs of many different stakeholders and thus many different sources of values. In a business dominated by one founder owner-manager it is relatively easy to define the values that predominate. They will derive from the personality of the founder, who often continues to rule the business with a rod of iron. Governance in such an organisation is difficult to separate from personal fiat: 'What I say goes, and stakeholders only have an influence, indeed are only *recognised*, if I choose to recognise them.'

But in an organisation that has passed through several stages of evolution; which has an established cadre of professional managers, many of whom have probably never even met the founder; which is located across many sites and geographies; which benefits from the support of a disparate group of financial investors; and which sells its services to a sophisticated group of professional buyers – is it possible to define one set of values at all? It is. Some of the most successful bigger businesses with strong values have managed to bottle the personal qualities that their founders once exhibited (or according to company legend exhibited) and convert them into organisational values, which in turn comprise a key element of an organisational culture that can be managed. But big companies do not need famous founders and well-documented histories in order to establish the values that matter the most to their organisations, and that define what might and might not be acceptable.

In order to make a value proposition work it has to infuse every aspect of an organisation. One professional service firm that takes values seriously will structure its appraisal documentation for partners and staff around its values. Structured interviews for potential new recruits are also organised around its values. When key issues trouble the partnership it is the values that are brought out to test them against. The values are engraved on the glass walls of the meeting rooms. Partners and staff cannot avoid them. They are as much a part of the governance framework as the partnership agreement and the management structure.

Many attempts have been made to demonstrate a connection between strong values in an organisation and performance. Jim Collins has built a career on it. 'Good to Great' used to be just a book. Now it is a website, a philosophy, an industry. His initial methodology involved a team of 21 researchers whittling down a list of 1,435 enterprises into 11 'rare and truly great' companies, and then exploring whether the winning team of 11 shared any characteristics. At the heart of all the companies, Collins asserted, was a corporate culture that rigorously found and promoted disciplined people to think and act in a disciplined manner.

There have been other attempts to identify a link. A venture between statistical researchers and surveyors ISR and accountants BDO started with a research project aimed at generating detailed insight into which values to foster (and how) in order to make fundamental and sustainable improvements to an organisation's commercial performance. Eight professional service firms and 2,000 staff participated in the survey. Initial findings again suggested that there are strong linkages between values and performance.

Scientific purists would blanch at the research methodologies of both these projects, but in part the lack of research rigour makes its own point: values work where measurement, methodology and logic (which collectively comprise the backbone of research) do not. The values proposition is intended to provide a set of tools to organisations that reach further than conventional measurement and incentive schemes. To cynics, of course, this smacks a little of religious fervour, which too often proudly associates itself with matters that are beyond reason, logic or proof. Cynics will also, rightly, argue that it is not just universally admired organisations that have strong value propositions and internal cultures. The same might be said of the Communist Party – or the Nazis.

But if you accept that values and culture have a part to play in governance, what should you do? First, you need to identify the particular values that underpin your firm. There are techniques for this, most of which involve pinpointing the elements that characterise the organisation via comprehensive staff surveys and workshops. Secondly, you should compare your values profile with the profiles that are likely to generate real performance improvement for you. Thirdly, you need to identify how to influence your values profile so that it moves towards that likely to yield performance improvement. This includes aligning your values proposition with its other faces – its brand in particular. This essentially is a change-management exercise, but unlike most change-management exercises this one will be soundly built on foundations that really matter to the people in your firm, and will therefore be far more likely to bite. Fourthly, you should re-examine and reconstruct if necessary key management practices in the organisation and ensure they reinforce the values proposition.

Because values propositions are so difficult to measure they are particularly easy to fake. There are lots of organisations that say they take their values propositions seriously, but do not. But fakery is something that is only too easily associated with governance in general. Managers complete checklists mindlessly agreeing to behave in this way rather than that way, but do not mean it. Directors make public announcements about quality and customer care, but everyone really knows that it is only new sales that matter. Staff are sent on diversity programmes and money-laundering awareness-raising sessions, but when they return to their desks, what really matters when they face up to those difficult decisions? At a 1999 conference on ethics and corporate boards one speaker (in his speech entitled 'What a CEO expects from a board') pointed out that:

> [a] strong, independent and knowledgeable board can
> make a significant difference in the performance of
> any company ... [O]ur corporate governance guidelines
> emphasise the 'qualities of strength of character, an
> enquiring and independent mind, practical wisdom
> and mature judgement ...' It is no accident that we put
> 'strength of character' first. Like any successful company
> we must have directors who start with what is right,
> who do not have hidden agendas and who strive to
> make judgements about what is best for the company
> and not about what is best for themselves or some other
> constituency.[74]

Fine words, that just happen to have come from Kenneth

Lay, CEO of Enron, a company that on paper at least was a model of corporate governance. For too many institutions, and not just Enron, too much governance is about complying with the letter rather than the spirit of regulation. This is evident every time an MP makes the headlines when he or she equates 'doing nothing wrong' with 'not breaking any rules' when claiming expenses for porn films, paper bags or gardeners, or when 'flipping' second homes. It goes further than this, however: taking values seriously is about complying with the spirit even if there is not any regulation.

Valuing contradiction

Consider an example. Values, like regulations, can conflict. One professional services organisation has the following four defined values:

- Taking personal responsibility

- Mutual support

- Honesty and integrity

- Strong and personal client relationships.

You do not need to be a lawyer to be able to see the potential conflicts and inconsistencies between these value propositions. The first two propositions set the responsibility for action and decision both with the individual and the group. Faced with a difficult decision, should an individual look for the mutual support one might assume his colleagues will be only too prepared to give, or should he just take responsibility himself? And if a dispute arises with a client over a professional matter involving the potential integrity of an important client's position, which value should prevail? Honesty and integrity, or the closeness of the personal relationship with the client? If these values statements are treated as legal propositions or regulations, they are unworkable. But they can be useful nonetheless, as influences – perhaps the most important influences – in a debate in the firm about any important matter. The inherent tensions between them, born out of their contradictions, will help the firm make far better sense of reality than a regulatory framework that must always seek to reduce reality and will always run the risk of running into a set of circumstances not previously foreseen, which questions the relevance of the regulation in the first place. Better the angry debate than the mindless application of a regulation (or mindful exploitation of an unforeseen loophole).

Social enterprises and charities, as has been noted already, can on occasion have problems with performance management and measurement where volunteers are involved. Not that they should therefore throw their hands in the air and surrender. Volunteers may prove difficult to measure – but they will respond to the levers of control that for-profit organisations often disdain. Values systems, credos, belief systems and suchlike will have much more influence on volunteers and in charities in general than in for-profit organisations. They have to in the absence of the levers that 'for-profit' organisations can rely on.

Partnerships are organisations in which values, organisational culture and other intangible elements have an important and often underestimated role to play in governance. Partnerships are organisations led by elected and appointed individuals with delegated management authority, but even in well-managed partnerships it is difficult for any one individual to get the upper hand, or at least for long. With so much competition at the top, partnerships are inherently divisive, but they cannot survive without consensus. Getting consensus in a partnership has been likened to trying to herd cats, but a good firm will reach consensus in the end, which will significantly reduce the risk of individual partners doing daft things.

Conversely, a partnership that seeks to introduce too much discipline as a mechanism for short-cutting the route to consensus runs the risk of excluding many kilowatts of brain power that might turn a dubious decision into a good one. Much has been made, for example, of the role culture and discipline played in the downfall of Andersen, the auditors of Enron. Many in the profession, including those perhaps envious of the firm's success, talked of its partners and staff as 'androids', suggesting in part that the firm recruited to type, and expected staff and partners to conform. The consequence ultimately was a culture in which partners and staff could participate in the destruction of 300 computer files and emails and more than a ton of documentation. In many other less efficient and profitable firms, staff and partners would, one hopes, have at least asked why, if not questioning whether, and eventually, and before it was too late, just said 'No'. Conversely, as the credit crunch matured and once mighty investment banks started falling over, commentators began lamenting the disappearance of the old partnership culture that used to dominate the banking industry, now long since replaced by the short-term, profit-target-driven culture more typical of listed companies. Goldman Sachs, who seem to have survived the crash better than most, have been frequently applauded for retaining elements of their old partnership culture notwithstanding their listing.

So for various reasons, a mature partnership structure is therefore not often the route for the single owner who wants to carry on calling all the shots. But neither will it lead to shredding skip-loads of important evidence; only a partnership that has actually turned into a corporate structure and has thrown away too many of the key collective and collaborative characteristics of partnership, warts and all, will find itself doing anything quite as foolish as that. The culture of a large partnership therefore is a product *of* the partners, not something that can be foisted onto the partnership by senior management.

Of all the characteristics of partnership culture, it is unlimited liability that has the biggest impact. Unlimited liability introduces a bond of considerable power between partners in a traditional unlimited liability partnership. If you know that the careless or negligent actions of one of your partners might cause you to lose *your* house, you think differently about your partner's business activities than you would do if she were a fellow director on the same board. 'If a partner of mine asked for a £10,000 loan, I would give it to him without question,' one partner in a major national partnership said to me once: I might have questioned his judgement, but certainly understand the sense of trust, engendered by partnership, that the comment startlingly illustrated. Take away unlimited liability between partners and you take away not just one of the defining qualities of partnership, but one of the key governance safeguards as well. This is something that partners considering the move to becoming a limited liability partnership need to be mindful of. Similarly, partnerships who have left the 20-partner threshold far behind, or who have already made the move to LLP status (or both), need to work hard on governance if they are to stand a chance of preserving the spirit of partnership.

9 | Transparency

'Whenever the people are well-informed, they can be trusted with their own government.'

Thomas Jefferson

On 7 January 2009 Mr Ramalinga Raju, founder and Chairman of Satyam, India's fourth-largest software services exporter, wrote to his fellow board members informing them of his role in India's biggest corporate scandal in memory. His letter was copied to the stock exchanges, and the news sent Indian equity markets plummeting, with Mumbai's main benchmark index tumbling 7.3 per cent. The Indian rupee dropped as well, and many observers felt the scandal was to blame.

Mr Raju, who founded Satyam more than two decades earlier and took it public in 1991, said that Satyam's profits had been massively inflated over recent years and that about $1 billion (£667 million) or 94 per cent of the cash on the company's books was fictitious.

The first thing that students learn when being initiated into the mysteries of double entry bookkeeping is to 'never argue with cash'. The cash balance in a set of financial statements is the fulcrum around which all the other numbers pivot. It is also a number that can be easily reconcilable to external sources of information – bank statements and certificates, for example. The last number that most fraudsters will tamper with on a set of financial statements therefore is the cash balance. Most frauds will happen before the cash gets reported. For the cash balances themselves to be fictional implies a failure of accounting reporting at a systemic level. Mr Raju's fantasy world began to fall apart at the end of 2008 after the company failed in its bid to buy two construction firms partly owned by members of the family, which Raju described as his final attempt to resolve the problem of the fictitious assets. 'It was like riding a tiger, not knowing how to get off without being eaten,' Mr Raju said in his letter. Like Bernard Madoff only a few weeks earlier, Raju seemed more than prepared to face up to the legal consequences of his dealings.

Raju warned his board members, presumably without appreciating the understatement, 'You may have a "restate-ment of the accounts" prepared by the auditors in light of the facts I have placed before you.' Mr Raju, understandably, did not remind his fellow directors that just three months before Satyam had received a Golden Peacock Award from a group of Indian directors for the excellence of its corporate govern-ance. And no doubt none of them needed reminding that 'Satyam' means 'trust', or 'truth' in Sanskrit. Some commen-tators were quick to point out that 'Satyam' was just Sanskrit for 'Enron'.

Mr Raju claimed that no other board member had been aware of the financial irregularities, which begs questions about the strength of the board and its oversight, as well as the role of the chairman. But we have discussed the role of the chairman already. Our subject in these paragraphs is infor-mation and its role in corporate governance. 'If a company's chairman himself says they built fictitious assets, who do you believe here? This has put a question mark on the entire cor-porate governance system in India,' said R.K. Gupta, Manag-ing Director at Taurus Asset Management in New Delhi.[75] It is more than a matter of irony that Satyam's services, principally outsourcing, included the provision of outsourced accounting and finance services.

Communication

Communication – the flow of information around a company, particularly to, from and between directors and shareholders; and the flow of information from the company to stakeholders – is a key subject for those responsible for corporate governance. It is through quality, timely information that those remote from the coalface can be protected against those close to the coalface, with their noses pressed against the data. Corporate governance gives attention to the quality of the information, its timeliness, the form in which it is presented and the responsibility of people for it.

The US Public Company Accounting Reform and Investor Protection Act of 2002, commonly called Sarbanes-Oxley, or just 'SOX' for short, was introduced as a hurried and controversial response to the failings and failures of Enron, Tyco International, Adelphia, Peregrine Systems and WorldCom amongst others, which cost listed companies in the US a fortune, and led to a surge of activity in accounting and audit firms. The Act was really all about communication, as a quick look at its provisions in outline demonstrates. SOX contains 11 'titles', as follows (with the italics drawing attention to the items relating to information and reporting):

1   **Public Company Accounting Oversight Board (PCAOB)**

    Established the Public Company Accounting Oversight Board to provide independent oversight of auditors. It also created a central oversight board tasked with registering auditors, defining the specific processes and procedures for compliance audits, inspecting and policing conduct and quality control, and enforcing compliance with the specific mandates of SOX.

2 **Auditor independence**

Established standards for external auditor independence, to limit conflicts of interest. It also addressed new auditor approval requirements, audit partner rotation, and *auditor reporting requirements*. It restricted auditing companies from providing non-audit services (e.g. consulting) for the same clients.

3 **Corporate responsibility**

Mandated that *senior executives take individual responsibility for the accuracy and completeness of corporate financial reports*. It also defined the interaction of external auditors and corporate audit committees, and *specified the responsibility of corporate officers for the accuracy and validity of corporate financial reports*. It enumerated specific limits on the behaviours of corporate officers and described specific forfeitures of benefits and civil penalties for non-compliance. For example, *Section 302 required that the company's 'principal officers' (typically the chief executive officer and chief financial officer) certify and approve the integrity of their company financial reports quarterly.*

4 **Enhanced financial disclosures**

Described enhanced reporting requirements for financial transactions, including off-balance sheet transactions, pro-forma figures and stock transactions of corporate officers. It required internal controls for assuring the accuracy of financial reports and disclosures, and mandated both audits and reports on those controls. It also required timely reporting of material changes in financial

condition and specific enhanced reviews by the SEC or
its agents of corporate reports.

5   **Analyst conflicts of interest**

Introduced measures designed to help *restore investor
confidence in the reporting of securities analysts.*

6   **Commission resources and authority**

Laid down practices to restore investor confidence in
securities analysts. It also defined the SEC's authority
to censure or bar securities professionals from practice
and defined the conditions under which a person can be
barred from practising as a broker, adviser or dealer.

7   **Studies and reports**

Required the Comptroller General and the SEC to
perform various studies and report their findings. Studies
and reports include the effects of consolidation of public
accounting firms, the role of credit-rating agencies in
the operation of securities markets, securities violations
and enforcement actions, and whether investment
banks assisted Enron, Global Crossing and others
to manipulate earnings and obfuscate true financial
conditions.

8   **Corporate and criminal fraud accountability**

Described specific criminal penalties for fraud by
manipulation, destruction or alteration of financial
records or other interference with investigations, while
providing certain protections for whistle-blowers.

9   **White-collar crime penalty enhancement**

Recommended stronger sentencing guidelines and
specifically *added failure to certify corporate financial
reports as a criminal offence.*

10 **Corporate tax returns**

Stated that the Chief Executive Officer should sign the company tax return.

11 **Corporate fraud accountability**

Identified corporate fraud and records tampering as criminal offences. It also revised sentencing guidelines and strengthened their penalties, which enabled the SEC to temporarily freeze large or unusual payments.

Sarbanes-Oxley only applies to listed companies. But private companies need to worry about communication too. Private companies also have stakeholders with differing interests and concerns at varying distances from the sources of quality information about the business. Corporate governance tries to manage the consequences of these asymmetries in information flow. In private businesses just as in listed businesses, directors in particular are in privileged positions and some find it only too tempting to abuse the power that knowledge brings. It is the directors of the company who are responsible for the company's financial statements, for example. To the uninitiated financial statements are statements of fact, but this is not the case. Notwithstanding thousands of pages of accounting regulation, and regardless of the attentions of auditors, all financial statements, good and bad, are tissues of judgements and subjective assessments. It is the directors who are responsible for the subjectivities, and with the best will in the world, directors will always be inclined to present information in a light that serves an interest that they can relate to. It is worth remembering when interpreting sets of financial statements that there are always two sets of stories to tease out – the stories that the directors are trying to tell, and also the stories the directors are trying to hide.

Complex reality versus helpful simplicity

Management and financial information also suffers from the syndrome already identified for rules and performance-related pay – the trade-off between the complexity that reflects reality, and the simplicity that is a characteristic of usefulness. Again, Einstein's dictum that things should be as simple as possible, but no simpler, is relevant here. But the best-known manual of Generally Accepted Accounting Practice, though shorter than the Companies Act, still comes in at 1,440 pages and weighs 1.8 kg. Those responsible for preparing accounts unsurprisingly need professional qualifications acquired over years of study as a result of which it can be assumed they have some familiarity with this weight of paper – though, as the regulations and guidance changes continuously, notoriously it is often only the newly qualified accountant who is likely to be fully up to date. But what of the recipient of financial information? Many readers are also qualified accountants; but by no means all of them, and certainly not all members of the diverse stakeholder group, sheltering under and seeking protection from the corporate governance umbrella, and trying to extract the stories the directors are trying to tell and the stories the directors are trying to hide. It is not really *that* surprising therefore when the businesses run by people like Madoff and Raju appear subsequently to have been described by financial statements that bear no relation to the reality, and that have pulled the wool over everyone's eyes, including quite probably their authors'. On the other hand, 'straight' sets of accounts are also doomed to perplex even the sophisticated. Just consider a little example chosen quite literally at random from the audited financial statements of a leading UK PLC:

163

The adjusted earnings per share figures have also been calculated based on earnings excluding the effect of property disposals and exceptional items. These have been calculated to allow the shareholders to gain an understanding of the underlying trading performance of the Group.

For diluted earnings per share, the weighted average number of ordinary shares in issue is adjusted to assume conversion of all dilutive potential ordinary shares. The Group has only one class of dilutive potential ordinary shares being those share options granted to employees where the exercise price is less than the average market price of the Company's ordinary shares during the year.

Notwithstanding the calm assurance of the second sentence of the first paragraph quoted, I invite you to submit your answers, on a postcard please – but only without consulting the handbook.

In the event of not being able to extrapolate from the financial statements either the story the directors are trying to tell or the one they are trying to hide, possibly because of a lack of required accounting knowledge – a state that is typical of most lay people, and only too common among even qualified accountants – many look to take comfort from the judgement of an authoritative third party, published or otherwise. Authoritative third parties include the auditors, but there are others. The credit-rating agencies also give some sort of comfort to external stakeholders about the health of the companies they rate, while investors and customers will also rely on the judgements of investment managers, brokers, journalists – and each other. But all of these, though better than nothing, can be disastrously wrong.

When a big company goes under the auditors are often the first in the firing line. Unsurprisingly, auditors were mentioned frequently in the Sarbanes-Oxley legislation – and they benefited a lot from the work this generated for them. Observers were quick to cry wolf when it was found out that the auditor of Bernard L. Madoff Investment Securities LLP was one Friehling & Horowitz, a Manhattan firm with one elderly partner based in Florida, an accounting assistant and a secretary. According to a nearby office worker, the accounting assistant turned up for periods of 10 to 15 minutes and then left. How could such a firm have the resource and the expertise to opine on the health of a business with assets supposedly in excess of $30 billion? At least one investment firm spotted the incongruence and cited this as a potential reason for warning its clients off Madoff funds. Learning on the job, journalists were also quick to set off in pursuit of the auditors of Sir Allen Stanford's business empire; their appetites quickened when the SEC were discovered describing them as a 'small, local accounting firm'. The founder of the London branch of C.A.S. Hewlett was found to have died the day after Stanford's year-end. His daughter and employee, who claimed not to know too much about presumably the firm's largest client, offered little comfort. The fact that the firm in the UK operated under licence from the Institute of Chartered Accountants of Antigua and Barbuda did not reassure much either. In both of these instances the palpable inadequacies of the auditors were rightly identified as fundamental flaws in their clients' governance regimes.

Big audit firms have also failed to play their part in preventing governance failures. It is too easy to pick out the stories that have made the biggest news – for example, Enron and Andersen, when a firm of auditors was considered by many to have been too close to the management of the company, and too involved in its choice of strategy, operating model and financial reporting to be able to report independently and objectively. But the truth is that all the major accounting firms at one time or another – and sometimes all at one time – have been on the wrong end of negligence claims from angry investors who have lost their money. They are angry because auditors do indeed provide a key element in any governance framework. Investors looking to blame auditors will express concerns about the quality of their work, and they will also question the independence of the auditors from management. In the UK it is the sharehold-ers who appoint the auditors, not the management, though in practice management are inevitably closely involved. In recent years audit firms have been required to rotate partners responsible for listed company audits, and the ability of the audit firm to earn non-audit fees from their audit clients has been much discussed. But auditors, even big ones, can fail to identify a governance failure. They can make mistakes. And a determined, fraudulent management team can on occasions find their way past their auditors. This risk will always exist.

In recent years credit-rating agencies have also received attention from aggrieved stakeholders. Joe Lieberman, Chair-man of the US Governmental Affairs Committee hearing into the fall of Enron, noted: 'On a *NewsHour with Jim Lehrer* program in 1996, *New York Times* columnist Tom Friedman went so far as to say – and I quote – "there are two super-powers in the world ... the United States and Moody's Bond Rating Service ... and believe me, it is not clear sometimes who is more powerful."'[76] Chairman Lieberman's comments on the credit agencies' judgements on Enron at the time of its failure are worth quoting at length:

> In the Enron case, I would have to conclude, that the
> credit raters appear to have been no more knowledgeable
> about the company's problems than anyone else who
> was following its fortunes in the newspapers ... After a
> summer during which Enron stock steadily declined, it
> was reported on October 22 last year that the SEC asked

the company to disclose its ties to outside investment
partnerships set up by the company's chief financial
officer. Enron's stock dropped 20 percent that day to a
closing price of $20.65 per share. On October 24, the
CFO, Andrew Fastow, resigned, and the stock dipped
to $16.41. Five days later, on October 29, Standard and
Poor's credit rating analyst appeared on CNN. By this
time, the agencies had put Enron on a 'credit watch',
but the company was still considered a good risk. The
Standard and Poor's analyst predicted that – and I quote
here – 'Enron's ability to retain something like the rating
that they're at today is excellent in the long term.' ...
When asked about the off-balance sheet partnerships,
the analyst assured investors that there would be no long
term implications. 'That's something that's really in the
past,' he said.

[At]... our last hearing ... a Wall Street analyst
testified that his 'buy' recommendation was supported
by the confidence expressed by the credit rating agencies
– which, he specifically pointed out, had access to inside
information about Enron's liabilities that he didn't
have. So, S&P's confidence had an effect on others. On
November 2, the S&P analyst once again expressed his
strong belief that Enron's off-balance sheet problems
were nothing to worry about. The analyst said S&P had
– quote – 'a great deal of confidence there are no more
surprises to come ... I think it is going to take a little bit
more time before everybody can get fully comfortable
that there is not something else lurking out there.' We
now know the market was not convinced. The stock
price continued its descent, dropping to $8.41 on
November 8, when Enron disclosed it had overstated
earnings by over half a billion dollars since 1997. Still,
the rating agencies kept Enron at 'investment grade'. By
November 28, the day Moody's and Standard & Poor's
downgraded Enron to junk bond status, the company's

stock was trading at just over a dollar. Four days later, of course, it went into bankruptcy. In other words, the credit raters – despite their unique position to obtain information unavailable to other analysts – were no more astute and no quicker to act than others.[77]

For their part the agencies have always been quick to point out that their ratings were 'opinions'. But the core sentence in an auditors report also starts with the key phrase, 'In our opinion ...'

Third-party certification, expressions of opinion and the silent hand of the market, taken in aggregate, all provide valuable assurance about the accuracy, veracity, reliability and transparency of the published accounts of a business. They all have key roles to perform in a governance framework. But as the Enron story shows, they can all get it horribly wrong.

At the heart of the Enron story is a determination on the part of the executives to hide the true story of the financial performance of the company. That they succeeded of course points to failures in the systems that supported the judgements made by the auditors and credit-rating agencies. It also points to an inability of prescribed accounting methodology to keep up with the increasingly sophisticated and Byzantine structures that were being devised to cover up the tracks of the directors. Above all it points to a determination on the part of some of the executives to have their tracks hidden.

The market itself provides a form of external 'certification' of a company's health, at least for a listed company, and thus contributes another element of governance. This was brought home strongly to me when, as a junior auditor, I was offered a lift to the tube station from a City dinner in the rain by a kindly gentleman in a limousine, who turned out to be the Chief Executive of a FTSE-100 company. He had been to the same dinner, and though he was kind enough to pay me some attention, the first thing his driver told him as he climbed into the car was the closing price of his company's stock on both London and Wall Street. It wasn't a time when either the bulls or bears were roaring in the markets, and as far as I was aware his business was under no particular pressure at the time, but his waking and sleeping moments seemed far more concerned with the tyranny of the markets than with the opinion of an auditor or the role of a regulator. And so, for many, it should be – particularly those for whom governance is all about safeguarding the interests of the shareholder; for what is a share price other than a snapshot comment on the company provided by its owners? And even if the points of view of individual shareholders are limited, in aggregate their views have meaning and influence (assuming they have not been distorted by short sellers).

Transparency on the part of the management of a business is thus a key element in any governance regime. 'Sunlight is said to be the best of disinfectants; electric light the most efficient policeman,' wrote Justice Brandeis.[78] But management will also always be under pressure to hide as well as to reveal. In parallel with the rise of the corporate governance industry has been the rise of the industries designed to safeguard and protect information. If governance depends on disclosure, competition (other than in the perfectly competitive world that exists only on the pages of a theoretician's textbook) depends on secrecy. Corporate espionage costs the largest thousand companies in the world $45 billion every year, according to one consultancy firm,[79] a sum big enough to concern anyone interested in the subject of corporate governance, including those interested in safeguarding shareholders. Even inside a business managers have to be careful about who they tell what. In the world of a listed corporation, a shareholder – an owner of the business, let us not forget – will be considered an outsider. Indeed, there are plenty of examples of outsiders (even enemies) of organisations who have sought to take advantage of the cover provided by share ownership to prosecute their own interests rather than, arguably, those of the company. What else, in the minds of management at least, is a hostile takeover bid? It is interesting, therefore, to note that much in the way of company regulation is not about openness on the part of management, but openness on the part of shareholders – particularly those that harbour an intent to take a company over.

We are once again reminded that governance is not just about 'protecting shareholders'. We're also reminded that, as with most things in governance, there is a hard-to-define balance that needs to be established here between transparency and secrecy, and trust and disclosure – a balance that will (indeed, perhaps must) be tested and threatened from time to time. As Samuel Johnson put it, 'It is better to suffer wrong than to do it, and happier to be sometimes cheated than not to trust.' This is unfortunately, or perhaps fortunately, as true of governance as it is of life. Indeed, the more complex a system the more important a role trust plays. Paul Seabright, an economist from the University of Toulouse, has noted that trust has evolved to the extent that people are more prepared to trust large sums of their own money to individuals they have never met than small sums of money to their next-door neighbours.[80] It is also a reminder of the human element in communication Research tells us that individuals are more likely to believe a message delivered face to face and by an immediate superior, than a message by memo from the CEO in a different city. The trouble with accounts, which are even more remote, is that they are not human, or believable. For too many they are not transparent – and they do not count as communication. In boom times, when the short-term temptations for the selfish greedy have more influence than the long-term benefits to be derived from safeguarding the interests of all, trust and transparency are invariably compromised. Between 1997 and 2000, before anyone had heard of Sarbanes-Oxley, and while Enron was winding itself up, 700 US companies were forced to restate their earnings. In 1981, just three companies did.[81]

10 | Growth and complexity

'I do not give a fig for the simplicity on this side
of complexity, but I would give my life for the
simplicity on the other side of complexity.'

Attributed to Oliver Wendell Holmes

Governance is of course an issue of concern for the very
biggest of businesses, but when, in the evolution of a business, does it become a concern?

In the beginning, governance is not a concern of the
business. In part this is because the youngest and smallest
businesses are not businesses at all, at least not in a sense in
which the business organisation can be separated from the
individual who is the business itself. A sole trader is not so
much a business as an individual in business. Governance
in businesses of this size has little to add to the management
of relations between shareholders and directors, though the
management of relations with other stakeholders is often
still an issue. But right from the beginning a key influence
on governance asserts itself: governance and management in
the owner-managed business is a very personal thing. Owner-
managers are far more likely to care. The business is an exten-
sion of themselves, and governance is something they take
personally or not at all.

Governance triggers

Governance first rears its head properly when founders become aware that the business they have put together is beginning to have a separate identify from themselves, and, in the case of joint founders, is beginning to be a source of tension between them. The story of a client of mine is illustrative. Founded by four colleagues made redundant at the same time, the business started, as many do, almost accidentally. As part of their termination arrangements the four friends were given a couple of client projects to complete. What started off as a redundancy payment in kind turned into a business. After trading for several years, by when the business was turning over several millions, the owners received an offer to buy the company. The offer was not solicited, nor did the founders need it, but the seed had been sown. One of the four definitely wanted to sell, but one of the others definitely did not. The remaining two did not know what they wanted, but they did know that, from that moment on, discussions between the founders were all about whether to sell the business or not, and not about the business itself. The founders had discovered that they had shareholder issues that needed managing just as they had management issues. They overlapped, but were not the same, and needed disciplines in place to make sure the issues did not complicate each other. This, for the founders, was a governance issue for real. The founders sought outside help assessing their options, and they ended up rejecting the offer; constructing and implemented a new strategy; and selling the business some years later for a much higher price.

The young business freshly equipped with external shareholders, often as a consequence of refinancing, finds itself at another point in its evolution when governance comes to the fore. Such businesses again appreciate one of the most important governance issues: the need to separate shareholder issues from operational management issues. Even businesses without external shareholders will appreciate the benefits of separating the discussions. This is not just about ensuring the formalities are observed when running statutory meetings of the shareholders with their panoply of ordinary, special and extraordinary resolutions, and concomitant notice periods. It is common in the younger owner-managed business for day-to-day operational issues to be lost in a discussion that is really about shareholder strategy. Issues of ownership are different from issues of management; the former is about investment and return, the latter about operational effectiveness and efficiency. The tension will become more apparent as the management team is expanded and investment issues become management issues. Delegating to new professionals is exceptionally difficult for many founders used to getting their own way. And sticking to disciplined meetings can be even more difficult for a business used to the creative chaos that is characteristic of being small, where key decisions are taken over a sandwich and 'strategy' is what happens down at the Dog and Duck. When the new finance director wanders past the CEO's office late on a Thursday night and sees the two founders arguing about something that was evidently too important for the agenda at that morning's newly instigated management meeting, it is easy for him question the importance of his own contribution.

It is good management practice – and good governance – to ensure that the business is managed by management that meets regularly as a team to consider reports on operational issues presented by managers responsible for the various areas. Meetings typically might be fortnightly or monthly. Meeting attendees need not be company directors as recognised by Companies House – an individual's attendance is justified if she is responsible for an area of business activity. Agendas should include standing items to ensure all key operational areas are reviewed thoroughly. Separate meetings of the board itself should be convened on a regular basis (though less frequently than the operational team) to receive reports from the management team, and also to consider matters of broader import for the business, such as issues put to shareholders. This separation of responsibilities might all seem a bit too big-business for some, but the discipline is useful for even the smallest businesses as a way of ensuring that agendas are not confused and interests do not conflict. A business in difficulty, for example, and dicing with potential insolvency is one in which it is particularly important for the owner-managers to appreciate the difference between their responsibilities as directors and their desires as shareholders. In such a business the interests of creditors wax just as those of shareholders wane. A shareholding director will benefit from the clarity that governance methodology will bring to thinking and decision taking.

If the founding owners are serious about new members in the management team, they have to be serious not just about changing meetings and management structure, but about changing the role they play themselves. No role changes more than that of the founders as the business evolves. 'I've seen entrepreneurs who embrace good people, and those who do not,' says one insider who has served as finance director with numerous growing businesses: 'The latter type of entrepreneur is foolish and needs help!' Getting help – particularly help that involves adding to the capability and capacity of the management team – is one of the earliest and most important governance challenges a young business will face.

Becoming a family business

Businesses turning into family businesses find themselves thinking about governance. What is a family business? It is a surprisingly difficult question to answer. There are many businesses owned and run by families that choose not to think of themselves as family businesses, and there are businesses in which family involvement remains just a faint trace in the archives that are determined to present themselves to the outside world and the internal world as family businesses. A family business is therefore almost impossible to define with the precision preferred by many academics. The best definition of a family business is a business that *thinks* it is a family business. Businesses that think this of themselves are likely to have histories tied up with the history of a family, or more than one family; and members of the family at one time or another are likely to have had operational and executive roles in the business. The family is likely still to exert some influence, if not the controlling influence, over the business and its outlook, and quite possibly, though not necessarily, it will have control over some, if not the majority, of the equity. However, sometimes this control will be hidden behind group structures, trusts and other mechanisms designed to provide the family with some semblance of privacy, stability or tax efficiency.

Family businesses, at least private family businesses, are not required to recognise governance codes. Yet the management and leadership problems confronting family businesses are just as complicated, if not more so, than those confronting business types that have governance foisted on them. As Montaigne notes, 'There is scarcely any less bother in the running of a family than in that of an entire state.'[82] They are more of a bother than their non-family counterparts because of the central role played by the families that own and often lead them, and the tensions between the emotion-based family values systems and the task-based values systems of the business. The two systems are essentially different, but the creation of a family business forces the two to overlap.

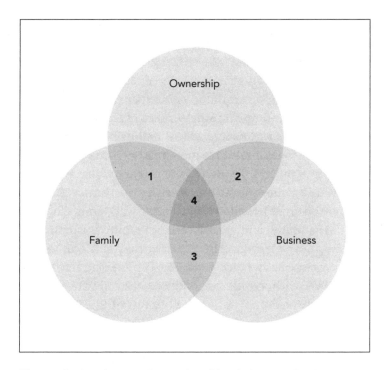

Figure 1 The 'three-circle' model of family business[83]

Notes: Many of the stakeholders directly involved in a family business will fall within one (and only one) of the seven sectors created by the three circles. It is the individuals who fall into more than one circle that are subject to particular tensions:

1 This sector is within both the family and ownership circles and therefore includes family members who own shares in the business but who are not employees.
2 Owners who work in the business but are not family members.
3 Family members who work in the business but do not own shares.
4 Owners who are also family members and employees of the business.

The family/business tension further complicates the owner/ manager tension common to all owner-managed businesses, leading to the well-known 'three-circle model' in which the independent but overlapping systems comprise the family, ownership and the business (see Figure 1). The tensions are at their most extreme at the fault lines created where the circles intersect. But stakeholders who sit comfortably only in one of the circles, seemingly far from the epicentre, will still be affected by the tremors, particularly if they choose to bury their heads in sand.

The tensions can be particularly acute not least because few family businesses set out to create them in the first place. Indeed, very few family businesses set out to become family businesses. Most business founders are just happy enough if they are able to establish a business. It is only after many years of trading – by which time errant brother Jack has settled into running the warehouse, and perhaps Junior and his sister are eyeing each other suspiciously, wondering who will inherit the shares, and longest-serving employee and finance director Martha is wondering whether they will ever recruit more professionally trained managers – that Dad realises he has inadvertently created a family business, in which different individuals occupy different positions in the three-circle model, and have differing expectations, and react differently to some of the key questions of management and governance.

For example, with regard to dividend payments, non-owning family members who work in the business (sector 3 in Figure 1) often take a very different view to their relatives who own shares in the business but who are not employed by it (sector 1). The former may favour cutting dividends in order to boost reinvestment in the business (and thus improve their career prospects); the latter may well want dividends increased to provide a better return on their investment. Indeed, they may well suspect their cousins of overpaying themselves at the expense of a decent level of dividend.

Other potential sources of tension and conflict are reflected in questions such as:

● Who should lead the business – a family member or a professional recruited from outside?

- On what terms should family members be allowed to work in the business? Is employment for family members an opportunity or a birthright?

- Who should own shares in the business – just family members? And if so, what is a 'family member'? Do in-laws count? And what happens after a divorce?

- When should some of the more distant shareholders be bought out?

- How are the roles of family members to be defined and evaluated?

- How are family members who work in the business to be paid?

- How can family employees be made truly accountable?

- Do all the branches of the family have access to the same opportunities and information?

The more people involved, the more generations that are tangled up in the business, the more the reliance on non-family and family members for skill and capital, the more complex these problems become, and the greater the need to do something about them, otherwise it is the business that will suffer, followed by the family itself. Businesses with huge potential often fail, not because of problems with the under-lying business model, but because of squabbling stakehold-ers, and few squabbles are ever as bitter or as dramatic – or as destructive – as those that go on in and around family businesses. Unsurprisingly, one piece of research suggests that only 13 per cent of family businesses will make it to the third generation.[84]

Professionalising the management

All businesses that have grown quickly will recognise the pains of professionalising the management team. Businesses about to embark on this particular stormy rite of passage face up to it with trepidation. Professionalising the management team is about management adopting new mindsets and attitudes. It is also, in many instances, about changing the management team itself.

The correct time for this rite of passage depends on circumstance. For some it is a question of size – numbers of employees or financial performance. But undoubtedly businesses can grow pretty large still led by a team that has yet to pass through professionalisation. For other businesses it is more a question of ownership. Certainly external financing or a listing on either the Alternative Investment Market (AIM) or the main market brings with it pressures for the management team that many were only too keen to walk away from when they put the business together in the first place. Financiers will demand safeguards, accurate financial reporting, a seat on the board, agendas, minutes, business plans. One of the demands of an external investor will often be a good, experienced chairman. The role of chairman is discussed elsewhere in this book, but in the context of the young business it is someone able to ensure that meetings are disciplined, and that operational management discussions are not confused with shareholder issues. Unsurprisingly, therefore, one of the key consequences of business change of this nature is that some serious questions are raised about the role of the founder. Used to getting their own way, founders now have to adopt a more consensual approach, and for many this is impossible. Professionalising the management team and the exit of the founder are for many businesses two sides of the same coin.

A business soon to lose its founder is a business soon to be without the personality that has got it this far. This presents another governance challenge. Organisational culture fills the gap vacated by the personality of the founder. Culture is just one abstract construct that needs to be managed, and as has already been asserted, is a key component in any governance framework. If organisational culture is to have a positive influence on governance it is best established early. Culture ties the organisation together internally, and brand is the way that culture manifests itself to the outside world. As marketing expert Simon Gulliford has observed, businesses do not have a choice as to whether or not they have a brand, but they do have a choice as to whether or not they manage their brand. Similarly, companies do not have a choice as to whether or not they have an organisational culture, but they do have a choice as to whether or not that culture has a positive impact on governance.

As a business grows it develops a life independent from its founders and its managers and has a corporate image that needs developing and maintaining both internally and externally. The business has a complexity that reflects the fact that an increasing number of stakeholders have an interest in it and expect to be heard by its directors. The business has responsibilities as employer, property owner, consumer, investment vehicle and producer. Again this means a fundamental change in the nature of the role of the directors: even if they founded it, their business is no longer theirs. It also has consequences for the governance agenda, which rapidly matures as the business adds layers of complexity and types of stakeholder. Relationships with financial stakeholders are more complicated and are likely to be the source of particular tension. For most businesses the move to a stock market listing and a move away from owner-managed status has the biggest impact on its attitude to governance. But running a business under the scrutiny of institutional investors is something that happens long before a listing, and is a very different experience from running it solely under your own scrutiny.

Attempts to professionalise the management team lead to the recruitment of senior managers with specialist skills – HR, marketing, operations, IT and so forth. But senior managers need departments to manage. The new managers – or 'directors' – are often allowed, if not encouraged, to build around themselves their own empires of expertise, until many a growing business finds that it has built an infrastructure that is effective and professional, but increasingly remote from the coalface. Furthermore, the existence of a new team of professionals gives line managers an excuse for paying insufficient attention to important areas of management responsibility that they were previously obliged to worry about personally. Just as the professionals find themselves remote from the bread and butter of the business, so those responsible for bread and butter find themselves remote from matters as critical as people policy and marketing strategy. A consequence of professionalising the management team is often to widen the gap between management and other stakeholders. Governance, which is in large part about transparency and securing lines of communication, helps to bridge the gap that professionalising the team has created.

English academic, historian and satirist Cyril Parkinson would see in this tendency evidence for what has become known as 'Parkinson's Law' – that work expands to fill the time available for its completion.[85] I have come across a business, taking this rule seriously obviously, where the managing director has refused to implement a budgeting process on the grounds that at the end of the year line managers will be encouraged to spend what is left in their budget, and that budgets are inherently wasteful. As a consequence all financial decisions, no matter how small, have to be referred to either the managing director or the financial director for personal approval – there is no other mechanism for financial management. Once again, governance is seen as something personal, but governance conceived this personally is a constraint on the future development of the business.

Addressing the balance can mean some degree of flattening the organisation, but it is really about focusing internal service functions on customer needs, reinvesting in the organisation's core competence and requiring senior management to re-equip themselves with a degree of expertise in people and IT management that they have lost as the business has developed. If managed successfully, a 'back to basics' programme such as this sees everyone win. General managers find themselves back where they should be – in charge of the business as a whole. Specialist managers find themselves contributing to the whole of the business, rather than isolated in functional silos – and contributing to the whole of the business is what many 'specialist' managers really want to be doing. Key to this process is the role of the managing director in ensuring the other senior members of the team do not step away from the coalface; that they add value to each other; that the human resources policy is presented internally as robustly as the business is marketed externally; and that IT systems are built and designed with people rather than IT specialists in mind. Key also is the role of governance: good governance will help tie the organisation together and keep communication channels open. Done badly, governance will help ensure management ossifies.

Ossification is the last thing any younger, owner-managed business needs. Notwithstanding professionalisation, members of the management team need to understand that their roles have to evolve as the business grows and develops. There is never one right way of doing any of the jobs at the top. There is only a way that happens to be right *now*.

Tomorrow the agenda will have changed. This may involve making some difficult decisions about people who were doing a good job last year but who are not going to be doing a good job next year. This also implies some coaching skills from the managing director or chairman, and it also gives plenty for a non-executive director to do. But of that, more later.

Growth and governance codes

The codes and frameworks recognise the influence growth has on the role governance plays in an organisation. As the Combined Code states in its introductory paragraphs:

> Smaller listed companies, in particular those new to listing, may judge that some of the provisions are disproportionate or less relevant in their case. Some of the provisions do not apply to companies below the FTSE-350. Such companies may nonetheless consider that it would be appropriate to adopt the approach in the Code and they are encouraged to do so.

Undoubtedly there is a presumption that governance is something that big companies need to worry about more than small companies. The Combined Code gives no attention to private companies at all, though some authorities have suggested applying its provisions to non-listed enterprises, as we discuss elsewhere.

Good Governance: A Code for the Voluntary and Community Sector, published in June 2005, comments more explicitly about size:

> We recognise that the language of governance and performance will be more familiar to larger organisations. In practice, the way organisations 'govern' will be different depending on the circumstances. These circumstances can include the size of an organisation,

how long it has been in existence, and the culture and values it possesses. One distinctive factor is size and here are a few examples of how an organisation's understanding of governance may differ:

- In a small community group governance might be about getting things in place, making sure it is clear who is doing what and making sure that all concerned are working together to a common cause.

- In a local or county-wide service-providing organisation, governance might be more focused on the relationship between the trustees and staff team, and ensuring good service delivery.

- In a larger national or regional organisation, governance might be about the need to demonstrate how the organisation delivers on its mission through quality service provision, its accountability to the public and stakeholders, and always ensuring that the board's structure is 'fit for purpose'.

The Code is written to be applicable in all such circumstances, but clearly each organisation will need to interpret and apply it according to its particular needs and circumstances.

Management and leadership

Some management writers[86] have drawn a distinction between creative, inspirational, enthusiastic types, and organised, disciplined, sensible managerial types, using the labels 'leader' for the former and 'manager' for the latter. The distinction has been usefully applied to entrepreneurs and other members of the management team.

Most businesses start high on leadership and low on management. If they are to stand a chance of developing into

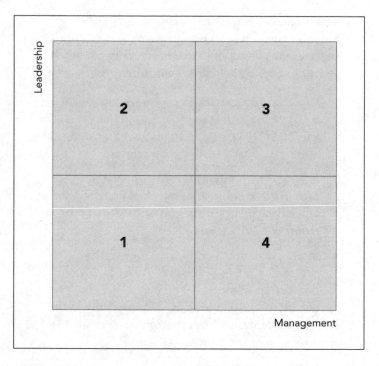

Figure 2 Leadership and management[87]

something that is remotely sustainable, then they will need more of those qualities of energy, inspiration and creativity. In terms of Figure 2, a business in its early stages will thus move from 1 to 2 if it is to evolve – dominated by individuals with qualities of 'leadership'. Governance in these early stages is as much a matter of force of personality as it is of anything else. But in these early stages the organisation as such hardly exists at all. The business is impossible to identify separately from its founder and owner, and good governance is perhaps better described as good behaviour.

But things change. As Jeremy Newman, now Chief Executive of BDO International, wrote:

New businesses are started by entrepreneurs who, through some combination of wisdom and luck, create and implement a successful business strategy. The business expands and profits grow and with this comes the need to hire professional managers. So people are recruited and promoted to manage, to cope with the growing bureaucracy and to prevent things getting out of control. And so the organisation grows and management grows to cope with it.[88]

The introduction of 'management' heralds reporting timetables, appraisal schemes, formal agendas and other manifestations of the way to run a 'proper' business. It also heralds more 'governance'. From an organisation that thrives on the petrol vapour of entrepreneurship and rushing around after the next sale, the new business inevitably evolves into one in which disciplined forces of management have far more influence. The business moves from 2 to 3. Of course 3, where leadership and management styles hold each other in balance, is the ideal position for the senior team to reach. ('Top right' is usually the place to be in all of these two-by-two boxes.) You want enough business discipline and governance to sustain the business, but not too much so that the qualities of entrepreneurship and leadership are damaged.

But for many businesses, staying 'top right' sounds good in theory but is difficult to achieve in practice. Some entre-preneurs ('leaders') see themselves as being obliged to turn into managers, or at least develop management capability. But although human beings can change and develop, rare indeed is the individual who can operate comfortably at both ends of the leadership/management spectrum. As the examples of Pessina, Iannou and others have already demon-strated, turning from an entrepreneur into a big business CEO or chairman is very difficult.

Rather than take the role themselves, other entrepreneurs might seek to ensure that management expertise is recruited and thus provided by others – allowing the entrepreneur the illusion of thinking that his role does not need to change that much. Unfortunately, old entrepreneurs and new managers have a tendency not to see eye-to-eye, and an unchanging entrepreneur is on target for serious conflict with a new management team, especially if it is comfortable talking the language of governance – which often results in the departure of one or the other, before or after damage to the business. Indeed, a reluctance to face up to the consequences of the tension leads some businesses to duck the problem in the first place. But businesses have no choice other than to introduce management infrastructure if they are serious about sustainable growth. Family businesses in particular, where blood is often thicker than mineral water, are particularly prone to deferring the necessary development of management. Managing the tension between entrepreneurship and responsibility is a key function of governance even when the business is large, as the Combined Code acknowledges: 'Good governance should facilitate efficient, effective and *entrepreneurial* management that can deliver shareholder value over the longer term.' The italics are mine, but the word is the Combined Code's.

Of course, the inference of this key sentence in the Combined Code is that, once established, the management force and some types of governance can do damage as well as good if allowed to get out of hand. The tendency for many with a managerial bent is to assume that the management force is more important than leadership, and entrepreneurial leadership in particular – indeed this is the natural tendency of much Western business thinking. As Jeremy Newman writes: 'This in turn stifles leadership and encourages management and because the business is successful, managers begin to believe that they are the best and their idiosyncrasies become part of the culture of the organisation.'[89] But whereas it is certainly true that a business without decent management will not survive for long, a business in which the management impulse takes over and squeezes the entrepreneurial spirit out of the organisation will turn into yet another over-managed, under-inspired, middle-aged business on a glide-path to history. This is box 4 on Figure 2.

Premature ageing in an organisation is almost as worrying as a refusal to let the organisation grow up. Such premature ageing is particularly a feature of 'start-ups' established by major blue chips, making the mistaken assumption that a small business is just a small version of a big one. I was once introduced to just such a start-up, founded as a stand-alone joint venture by two major PLCs. The new MD was keen to talk about 'establishing an entrepreneurial culture' but in the same meeting anxious to discuss implementing a defined benefit pension scheme – a sure sign of a business on its way to being old before its time. In this context I find it interesting how many finance directors succeed the entrepreneur as chief executive in maturing businesses. It is as if the discipline of accountancy has superseded the energy and creativity and propensity to take risk that used to be embodied in the person of the founder entrepreneur.

Hence the need in big businesses for governance to allow room for leadership – and to 'facilitate' entrepreneurship. 'Managing winds up being the allocation of resources against tasks. Leadership focuses on people,' argued Carol Bartz, the CEO of Yahoo! 'My definition of a leader is someone who helps people succeed,' she went on to say.[90]

As well as highlighting a contrast between the entrepreneur and more managerially and governance-minded members of the team, the leadership versus management model outlines what is for many businesses a key feature of the history of their growth and development. All businesses have to pass through stages in their evolution, and the managerial, organisational, strategic, operational – and governance – imperatives differ significantly from one stage to the next. In short, as well as growing, businesses have to grow up. Growth is all about change, and governance mechanisms therefore have to change as well. This is difficult for governance mechanisms, which often seek security in stability.

Businesses grow up at different ages and different sizes. The Combined Code imposes obligations on listed businesses, FTSE-250 companies in particular, which has the effect of ensuring that all businesses adopt the same standard of governance at the same stage of evolution. But up to that point governance arrangements are much more flexible, and reflect the attitudes of shareholders and management. In companies that grow slowly, governance mechanisms can evolve slowly and through trial and error. Companies that grow quickly have no such luxury. Governance mechanisms – and other facets of the management system such as HR, marketing and finance – are more likely to be bolted on in response to crises; and will need to be modified in fairly short order as the business develops still further. On the other hand, some aspects of the governance system will be left behind. A business that has grown quickly might find itself with a finance director who has done a good job getting the business to where it is, but little idea of how to take it further. On the other hand, it might already have the benefit of a couple of good non-executive directors.

What in effect we are demonstrating is that business development and evolution bring increases not just in scale but also in complexity, and governance mechanisms have to be able to cope with different types of complexity as well. There is a correlation between complexity and scale, but it is only a correlation. There are plenty of small businesses where complexity is a key characteristic of the business model.

Growth	Pressure for performance		Rate of expansion		Inexperience of employees	
	?	+	?	+	?	=
Culture	Rewards for entrepreneurial risk taking		Executive resistance to bad news		Level of internal competition	
	?	+	?	+	?	=
Information management	Transaction complexity and velocity		Gaps in diagnostic performance measures		Degree of centralised decision making	
	?	+	?	+	?	=

Figure 3 Risk exposure calculator

Source: Simons, R. (1999) 'How risky is your company?',
Harvard Business Review

Harvard Business School professor Robert Simons has proposed an interesting framework for assessing in summary form the business risk faced by a company, which also in effect captures the complexity inherent in the business.[91] The 'Business Risk Calculator' – tested, according to Simons, by 'managers from hundreds of different companies' – invites managers to categorise and assess the extent to which their business is exposed to each category (see Figure 3).

Taking the first line in the figure first, the questions here relate purely to growth. To what extent are managers and staff under pressure to deliver? How fast is the company growing anyway? To what extent do managers and staff have experience of the situation in which the business finds itself? Give your company a score, and the higher the number the greater should be the alarm. High scores across this line indicate a company that might be growing and changing more quickly than the capability and capacity of management to control it.

The second line assesses some of the softer elements in a governance framework. How significant are the potential rewards for risk taking that are waved in front of staff? How resistant are executives to receiving bad news? ('Do not give me problems, bring me solutions!') How competitive is the internal environment? High scores across this line might suggest that individuals could be more likely to take risks than is good for the company, and that the same individuals are less likely to draw problems to the attention of management in time for management to address them.

The third line is about complexity. How fast does the business engine that underpins the business turn over, and how many components are in the engine? The more there are, the less likely that management is going to be fully aware of the business. To what extent do the performance indicators chosen to measure performance capture the totality of activity in the business, or are there fundamental gaps? How decentralised is decision taking in the business? Have controls been put in place to supervise the managers to whom authority has been delegated, or have senior management in effect confused delegation with abdication?

All three of the lines in Figure 3, and each item within each line, interlock with each other. High numbers across the board suggest a business that is growing fast, getting more complicated and not under the control of management. Simons proposed his model in 1999, but his lessons have not been taken to heart. Apply this framework to Lehman Brothers or RBS as they both galloped through 2006 to 2008 and see how many low scores you can find.

11 | Structures and power

'Experience hath shewn, that even under the best forms [of government] those entrusted with power have, in time, and by slow operations, perverted it into tyranny.'

Thomas Jefferson

The Head of the Treasury in Upper Egypt, Old Kingdom, c. 2200 BC gave himself the title of 'The Governor of All That Exists'. Just to be on the safe side he added, '... and All That Does Not Exist'. The historian who notes the title does not record what Pharaoh made of this, but evidently the distribution of power among the senior members and officers of an organisation has always been a controversial matter for big egos in particular.[92]

Structures, especially management structures, have a key role to play in any governance framework. Who reports to whom, and what checks and balances are in place on the authority and power of the key decision takers, are critical governance issues.

Governance and authority

All organisations since the abolition of slavery have to be a blend of autocracy and democracy. I have already described small, entrepreneurial businesses as benevolent dictatorships. The organisation chart of an entrepreneurial owner-managed business will often resemble a spider's web, with all reporting lines converging on the founder. A non-executive director friend of mine observes that one of his first jobs in a young business is to 'unplug' one end of these reporting lines and re-plug them into newly created middle management, to which the owner-manager should delegate significant areas of his responsibility. This in itself is an act that constrains the power of the founding team, and it is an act that many entrepreneurs find difficult. 'If you want something done properly around here, you've got to do it yourself,' is a line I often hear from entrepreneurs. 'We have too few good managers,' is another. 'What we really need is someone else like me,' is a third. All three of these statements betray an individual determined to hang on to too much authority for too long.

To some extent, even the most authoritarian of business leaders can only lead their staff where they wish to be led. Staff are paid, and this gives leaders significant leverage (though the ability to influence staff through performance-related pay is in my opinion somewhat exaggerated: by and large performance-related pay mechanisms are implemented by leaders who like them for the benefit of staff who do not). But key figures in some organisations – charities and not-for-profits in particular – are volunteers, and thus beyond the reach of the control mechanisms that even if only notionally apply to paid staff. Additionally, at the top of any organisation there have always been, and will always be, individuals ambitious enough to exert more influence than the titular chief executive or chairman wishes to cede. At the same time, however, staff have to accept that their organisations are not democracies as understood in political theory. The governors of a business are not accountable to the governed in a business in the same way they are in a democratic state. Management might seek to 'consult' their staff on matters of strategy; they might even be compelled to do so by legislation when faced by some employment issues such as potential redundancies, but it is still management who take the decisions. The fact that staff might organise themselves into democratic organisations that run in parallel to the organisation they work for (such as trades unions) suggests that staff have on occasion felt their channels of influence within the organisation itself to be insufficient.

It is not just small businesses that suffer from the syndrome of the leader who is inclined to overreach his authority. I have already discussed (in Chapter 4) the matter of combining the roles of chairman and chief executive and noted it is a practice frowned upon in the UK at the least, and specifically discussed in the Combined Code. In America, the notion of the powerful chief executive has long held sway. When times go well they are heroes, their strategies are written up as business school case studies, and they are paid huge sums of money. When times are bad it seems they can do no right – and too many are accused of being tyrannical bullies, surrounding themselves with 'yes men', if not up in front of a grand jury for an offence that in essence involves an abuse of the powers entrusted to them by both board and shareholders. Alex Dalmady, the financial analyst who drew attention to potential matters of concern at Stanford International Bank, noted of its eponymous founder that one trait of most financial frauds is that 'there are few people (or only one person) overseeing everything'.[93] Those people who oversee everything are often colourful characters. Sir Allen Stanford, launching his sponsorship of his cricket tournament, landed at Lord's cricket ground in a gold-painted helicopter bearing millions of dollars. Bernie Ebbers, with a basketball scholarship and Bachelors degree in physical education (after twice dropping out of college), rose from humble beginnings to be the much-feted chief executive of WorldCom, a member of the Mississippi Business Hall of Fame and the holder of two honorary doctorates (including a doctorate of law). His management style was famously informal – meaning that there were very few records of decisions. But there is lots of testimony to his aggressive management style. He is currently serving 25 years for fraud and conspiracy for his role in the $11 billion fraud that led to the collapse of WorldCom in 2002, which lost 20,000 staff their jobs and shareholders some $180 million.

Picking on the fraudulent is perhaps easy when discussing governance failures in the context of leadership. The case of Richard Fuld, CEO of Lehman Brothers, is more interesting. Fuld again in his heyday could do no wrong, and even when things turned bad there was not a hint of a suggestion of any fraud. An MBA and a lifelong Lehman Brothers employee, Fuld was named the number one CEO in the industry in 2006 by *Institutional Investor* magazine. A year later his salary was $51.7 million, topped up in due course with a bonus of $22 million. Totally dedicated to the Lehman cause, hard-working and committed, Fuld possessed many admirable qualities as a business leader. Unfortunately, Fuld also just happened to be wrong about some particularly important matters, investing in mortgage-backed derivatives long after everyone else was pulling out, and turning down offers for his business because he thought they undervalued it. Fuld was also famously tough – too tough – as a boss. His Wall Street nickname was 'the gorilla'. When in the Air Force he got into a fist fight with his commanding officer. 'When I find a short seller I want to tear his heart out and eat it before his eyes while he's still alive,' he told an investment banking conference in the spring of 2008.[94] He was also convinced that his way was right and was determined to get it. 'His was the textbook example of the command-and-control CEO,' Lehman Brothers' Head of Communications and ex-editor of the *Financial Times*, Andrew Gowers, has written.[95] His chief aides' role was 'not to encourage debate or intellectual curiosity in subordinates but to bend the bank to Dick Fuld's will'.

Different again is Sir Fred Goodwin, CEO of RBS, who ultimately took the bank into its fated acquisition of ABN-Amro. It is a difficult and ultimately futile exercise to establish the extent of Sir Fred's responsibility for RBS's problems in 2008. What is evident is that catastrophic decisions were taken; the decisions were championed by Sir Fred as CEO, there were insufficient checks and balances to test the decisions and Sir Fred would not have taken such challenges lightly. It is also to be noted that the acquisition of ABN-Amro was voted for by 96 per cent of the bank's shareholders when the credit crunch was already picking up steam, and the FSA allowed the bank lower capital adequacy requirements in order to do the deal. Men such as Goodwin do not fit easily into a corporate governance system of checks and balances, nor do they easily accept other powerful individuals at the top of the companies they lead, but it is evident that a lot of people and institutions made it easy for him to take the wrong decision.

Nor is it just a case of separating the role of CEO and chairman. Yes, Bernie Ebbers held both roles at WorldCom as did Dick Fuld at Lehman Brothers, but the role is and was split at the top of RBS. Nor is it just a matter of finding softer individuals, more likely to take counsel from others, for the role of CEO. The role of CEO in a big business is as challenging a role as any, placing significant demands on its holder, physically, mentally and emotionally. These are big roles for big people. But individuals make mistakes. Good governance is in great part about ensuring that capable people focus their skills and energies in the right ways on the right problems, and such focus is far more likely to be achieved through structure, process, accountability and discipline – and by a prepared-ness to see the power of any one individual circumscribed. As Andrew Gowers notes when writing of Dick Fuld and Lehman Brothers again:

> Here was a corporate governance structure almost pre-programmed to fail: an over-mighty CEO, a top lieutenant eager to please and hungry for risk, an executive team not noted for healthy debate and a power struggle between two key players. Furthermore, the board of directors was packed with non-executives of a certain age and woefully lacking in banking expertise. It is small wonder that Lehman was so ill-equipped to recognise and adjust to the changes in the environment ...[96]

Hierarchies and control

The ability of an executive – chief or otherwise – to exercise power in his or her business is dependent on the structure of reporting lines and the extent to which the executive's will can be exercised without let or hindrance up and down those lines.

An executive can rule by command and edict or she can facilitate a more participative decision-taking process. As the recession of 2009 deepens, the second approach is more fash-ionable.[97] But a mindset that associates management and gov-ernance with discipline, obedience and compliance is still a useful mindset. Indeed, there are many who would argue that in a real crisis, when time is in very short supply, and difficult decisions are called for, and notwithstanding my comments above about Dick Fuld, a command and control culture with an authoritative leader figure at the top stands a better chance of delivering success than a more consultative, reflexive, self-challenging model. In times of crisis there just is not time for this sort of stuff. Talking is for when times are easy. The tough get going when the going gets tough.

Top-down, hierarchical management is easy to understand and easy to communicate to a new member of staff. It is tidy, efficient and logical. The boss bosses and those underneath do what they are told. Every individual knows who he reports to. Reporting lines are clear and unambiguous. Spans of control and territories are rigorously defined and enforced. The apotheosis of this approach was reached in Frederick Taylor's *Scientific Management*.[98] Taylor was a mechanical engineer and it shows in his thinking about management. All business activity can be rationalised, and tasks can be analysed and segregated. Individuals can be allocated to specialise in one task within the mighty machine and trained to do the task spectacularly well – as measured by his key performance indicators. The carrot of performance-linked remuneration can help them point in the right direction; the threat of sanction or even dismissal can encourage them to run in that direction just that little bit faster.

Taylor made no attempt to hide his suspicion as to what would happen to the average worker if left, foolishly, to his own devices:

> There is no question that the tendency of the average
> man [sic] (in all walks of life) is toward working at a slow,
> easy gait, and that it is only after a good deal of thought
> and observation on his part or as a result of example,
> conscience or external pressure that he takes a more
> rapid pace.[99]

Taylor's world-view makes little room for trust or delegated responsibility or consultation. But it has a lot going for it. To be fair to Taylor, many younger businesses are not nearly scientific enough in their approach to business organisation, and a dose of Taylor would do them no harm at all. Many new managing directors rightly start with drawing up an organisation chart, identifying who is supposed to be focusing on which job. A set of outline job descriptions can help enormously to clarify the organisational structure now that it is bigger – and a dose of pain and gain is a good way of influencing change. Also, the mechanical mentality, and the rule-sensitive, suspicious frame of mind it fosters, fit well with many people's notions of governance. It is a relatively small step from Taylor to some of the definitions of governance described in Chapter 1: 'The framework of rules and practices by which a board of directors ensures accountability, fairness, and transparency in the firm's relationship with all its stake-holders ...'

But such an approach to management has significant drawbacks too. An analytical, highly mechanised approach will create an efficient system in which all the cogs run smoothly. But in so doing it will create a system that is very difficult to change. Change one cog and the others will have to adjust as well – and in a mechanical set-up the cogs will be even less willing to change than normal. Forced to specialise, trained to do one thing very well, they are just not conditioned to do anything as radical as 'adjustment'. And in younger, growing businesses in particular, which claim strategic advantage through their ability to react, and which will need to change anyway as they grow (and grow up), organisational flexibility is absolutely critical. Such flexibility can best be assured if the cogs are allowed to determine their own destiny, adapting it to circumstance. Such an approach makes very 'unTaylorist' assumptions about humankind. For example, many would be reluctant nowadays to assume that 'all men' (it was only men that Taylor was interested in) are programmed to work at a 'slow, easy gait' and tend towards the idleness that this implies. The Taylor approach also has consequences for the top job. Under Taylor, the managing director is field marshal – or at least chief of staff. Under a bottom-up approach, however, the managing director is chief facilitator, the architect of a system that allows the individuals working with him (rather than for him) freedom to express themselves. When accused of being the boss or the leader, the managing director will talk of 'upside-down management', and the client-facing staff being at the 'top' and him at the 'bottom'. Or he will, at least, nod in agreement at the words of the Kris Kristofferson character in the 1978 film *Convoy*: 'I'm not the leader, I'm just the guy up front.'

Things are different when businesses are small. Most businesses start by being decidedly top-down dictatorships – and not necessarily benign ones either. On the other hand, small businesses also have the luxury of flexibility. Only when a business is small can flexibility and command-and-control easily coexist. The function of individuals within the business is unlikely to have been regimented or formally analysed. In the spirit of all dictatorships the business is run not by application of the rule of law or even sensible business process, but at the whim of the founder, who will know and be known pretty well by every member of the organisation. This is discipline, but quite a long way from the discipline of scientific management. But as the business grows and the personal influence of the founder gets diluted, aspects of scientific management are almost inevitably implemented to plug the gap. Staff will be set targets; there will be attempts at performance measurement; and individuals will be held accountable. Businesses, even small businesses, that depend on complex project management for success – an office move, or the development of a new, business-critical piece of software, for example – find that a disciplined, analytical approach is also central to successful project completion, on time and on budget. Indeed, key to any project implementation programme is the role of 'OMRB' – the 'one, mean, rotten bastard' whom everybody loves to hate but who is critical to the project. Frederick Taylor no doubt knew and approved of many OMRBs in businesses big and small. Staff in Enron, WorldCom and Lehman Brothers no doubt knew a few too.

Undoubtedly governance as most people understand it fits more easily with the inflexible, rule-based world that Taylor imagined. Much of the impatience many entrepreneurs express with governance is founded on a presumption that governance mechanisms will restrict, slow down and stiffen decision-taking processes and render them less fit for the fast-moving modern world. Alternative conceptions of management have come from other sources as well, and have in recent years put management in a very different relation to governance. The boss as more modest individual, more interested in a broader constituency of stakeholders, has been catching on of late. For Jim Collins in *Good to Great*,[100] 'level 5' leadership is a peculiar combination of professional will and personal humility. Ricardo Semler claims, when looking for new executives in his industrial equipment business, Semco SA, to work with the formula (IQ + EQ + SQ) – EGO = the ideal candidate (i.e. where EQ is a measure of 'emotional intelligence' and SQ is a measure of 'spiritual intelligence').[101] Of course you need the intellectual and emotional quotients. The need for 'spiritual quotient' might take some by surprise. But most important of all is the warning about candidates with too much ego. The title of a *Harvard Business Review* piece says it all: 'The curse of the superstar CEO'.[102] The fashionable boss is a quiet, self-effacing type of guy. This sort of management style presents a very different governance challenge to the Taylorist and hierarchical approach to management.

The hierarchical approach has other challenges. Businesses can no longer just give up being flexible when they get bigger, and hierarchies find it tough to meet the challenge. A hierarchy is difficult to change quickly and can be exposed if the pace of change in the environment accelerates.

Communication along the long reporting lines is inclined to be slow and subject to the 'Chinese whispers syndrome', so that the message that finds its way to the top is different from the one that left the bottom. And for every official hierarchy there is an unofficial one – the one that includes such positions as 'owner of photos from last year's Christmas party', and 'secretary who secretly runs the whole shooting match'. These unofficial roles are just as influential, and serve to prevent the official hierarchy from working effectively (though cunning managers take advantage of them).

To be fair, hierarchical management has been rethought in recent years, and there are those who have made a convincing case in favour of hierarchies. An interesting piece in the *Financial Times* made a case for the balanced hierarchy.[103] It reported on 'hierarchy value analysis', the latest technique for establishing whether your hierarchy adds value or subtracts it. The case 'for' is made gingerly. Managers, we are told, tend to overvalue their own importance, and undervalue that of subordinates. There is a natural bias towards over-managing. Unsurprisingly, we're recommended to avoid hierarchy unless its value-add exceeds its cost. Everything should be delegated to the frontline unless there is a good reason and all companies should be broken into independent business units unless there is a good reason for the units to share a common parent. But notwithstanding all the caveats, hierarchy is given a place in the management firmament. Besides, staff quite like hierarchies even though they will argue differently. 'Hierarchies show us how fast we are climbing the ladder to success ... hierarchies fulfil our deep needs for order and security,' argues Stanford Business School professor Harold Leavitt.[104] Again it is easy to see how a hierarchical approach fits in more easily and comfortably with standard notions of governance. On the other hand, the stories told earlier about WorldCom and Lehman Brothers in particular show how hierarchical management can foster a climate in which governance structures are almost bound to fail.

The cultures of other structures

As has been noted already, hierarchies are a lot easier to define, describe and run than many of the alternatives. Under 'matrix management' structures an individual will find himself reporting in several directions simultaneously. A departmental HR manager, for example, will report to the general manager responsible for his department – but will also report to the director of human resources at head office. This is difficult to describe and can be difficult to experience in practice as well, as different bosses with contradictory edicts compete for the attention of junior staff, who can be left confused or just amused depending on their temperament. Statements to the effect that the confusion reflects the 'richness' of problem solving in real business life and makes it more likely that the real issues will get identified, or that reporting lines can be prioritised by relegating some of them to the status of 'dotted', do little to clarify matters. However, there are specific circumstances to which such matrices, for all their problems, are suited. A business segmented by product and geography is complicated, and a structure that oversimplifies business reality will struggle to succeed in the long term.

Another fashionable alternative to the hierarchy that is more a reflection of culture than structure is the 'network' in which, taking advantage of IT both metaphorically and in reality, everyone 'reports' to everyone else. Again this is easier to reduce to an illustration than to make the basis of an approach to management and governance.

Many businesses find themselves caught in the middle as hybrids, with elements of both the traditional, Taylorist hierarchy, and more modern, fluid structures. Some organisations have a traditional hierarchy at the top of the organisation and a far more 'modern' consensual style at the bottom. There are bottom-heavy, management-light organisations that fit into this category. Then there are organisations such as many professional partnerships, with flexible, network-style structures at the top (the partnership) but a more traditional hierarchy for staff at the bottom. These types of structures can be an effective way of having your cake and eating it – of achieving the flexibility and speed of response of the one and the discipline and control of the other. But there will always be a rung of management who find themselves caught in the middle, trying to manage one way while experiencing management the other. Many managing directors tell a good story about the importance of collaboration and teamwork, but have suspect team skills themselves. Indeed, in bigger businesses you are most likely to find the route to the top if your elbows are sharp and your competitive instincts are well defined. You may well get to the top at the expense of your team-mates rather than thanks to them. Individuals caught in the middle between hierarchies and flat structures are in a very difficult position and often find the conflicting demands on their attention even more difficult to cope with than the demands placed on them under a matrix structure. Again, such structures have distinctive governance challenges.

Partnerships – ancient and modern?

Partnerships, as noted already, with their flat and flexible structures, for many are the model for organisations of the future. Yet the regulation governing partnerships dates right back to the 19th century. Modern partnerships that take their futures seriously do not just rely on the 1890 Partnership Act, which is the starting point for governance arrangements for partnerships; they will invest time and energy in drawing up a partnership agreement. (For partnerships that do not make their own arrangements, provisions set out in the 1890 Partnership Act will usually cut in by default.) Partnership agreements do for partnerships what memoranda and articles of association do for limited companies – but they go much further. In including provisions governing remuneration, partnership voting mechanisms, provisions for capital, good leavers and bad leavers, partnership agreements are also akin to shareholder agreements.

Partnerships are flat at the top, and many of the most important decisions are often put to the vote of the partners. Elections are a characteristic feature of partnership governance. In theory, elections feature in incorporated entities as well; after all, the shareholders vote on key issues, and directors around the boardroom table will raise their hands to show whether or not they are for or against a particular decision. But because the owners are the managers *and* the financiers in most partnerships, and because partnerships are inherently flat organisations, voting is far more a part of the fabric of partnerships than it is of limited companies. Indeed, some larger partnerships will make sure they continue to force votes on their partners for longer than might be argued necessary for the sake of effective decision taking, just to help reinforce the culture of partnership. Nevertheless what partners are allowed to vote on and what not are issues that need to be resolved if the right balance is to be struck between good governance and efficient decision taking. How to determine voting rights is also an important issue. Some decisions might best be settled by an election based on head count, while others might best be weighted to reflect the economic interests partners have in the business. Some decisions might need a simple majority, others a 75 per cent majority, some maybe unanimity. Unfortunately democracy has never been simple; nor is partnership.

Of course partnerships that grow will get to a size when it is no longer possible for all the partners to manage the partnership. Although the partners might get sentimental about the days when they could (and did) all meet around the same table every morning to open the post, they will recognise reaching a stage when management needs to be delegated. Who sits on the senior executive committee is a matter that will exercise all partners, particularly those who fondly remember the days when all partners were involved in every decision. It is a mistake, however, to presume that the members of the executive should each be elected by the partners. An executive needs to operate as a team, and although elections are quite good at picking individuals, they are not very good at picking teams – indeed there is a danger that a group elected individual by individual will fail to turn into a team at all. The US president picks his cabinet, as does the UK prime minister. So should a managing partner.

How the executive team is configured depends on the partnership's commercial objectives. Some will choose for the executive to reflect the firm's client service lines; others might choose to configure the executive more in line with a company board, with a head of finance, marketing, HR and so forth. The former will help ensure central management is aligned with the service lines in the business, while the latter will foster a climate in which an organisational infrastructure and professional support functions can be established and developed, but will run the risk of distancing management from client management. Indeed, the distance between central management and client activity is an issue that much exercises many large professional service firms. Managing any big business is a demanding task, and partnerships are no different. To many it is inconceivable that the key management roles should be anything other than full-time commitments. But finding a professional who wants to give up his or her profession for management is rare. Bringing in a 'professional manager' from outside certainly allows the partners to focus on professional activity, but runs the risk of central management not retaining credibility. Besides, in the increasingly risky world of professional practice it is important that central management is not just close to key partnership activity but on top of the key client decisions. The central figures in a partnership are usually not titled chief executive or chairman, but managing partner or senior partner; they are thus in partnership with their partners, not removed from them. Increasingly, even in the biggest partnerships, senior management retain client-facing roles, including often portfolios of clients.

Nonetheless some themes we observe in other structures still apply to partnerships. It continues to be important for management to be accountable. For too much power to be concentrated in the hands of any one individual can be as troublesome in a partnership as in any other entity – more so given that partnerships are essentially flat networks of individuals sharing commercial, professional and financial interests and risks rather than hierarchical personal fiefdoms. Partnerships might not be required by law to rotate their senior managers out of office, but should be wary of providing till-retirement-do-us-part arrangements for them. Just as a chairman might be separated from and provide a check on a chief executive, so might a senior partner be separated from and provide a check on a managing partner. Indeed, in some partnerships the senior partner takes the role of 'chairman' of key partnership forums – including meetings of the executive and meetings of the partnership as a whole.

Large partnerships also often institute separate governance mechanisms for looking after the equity interests of partners, as opposed to supervising the commercial interests of the business. A 'partnership council' might look after such matters as partner admission, partner discipline and in some instances partner remuneration. Such a council has elements of a remuneration or nominations committee. The council in some ways is analogous to the family councils found in large family businesses, and also serves the purpose of representing the interests of the 'owners' to management.

Flexibility through groups

Many large organisations attempt to achieve a balance of flexibility and discipline, control and decentralisation using group structures. Discrete business units can be established in individual companies. Sub-groups of related companies can be put together, and a series of sub-holding companies used at the same time to coordinate activity across the group and foster a spirit of delegation. Tax and other regulatory matters might well influence group structure, but organisations will be left very much to their own devices as to how decisions are taken, the interests of the various stakeholders respected and other governance matters addressed. Many if not most groups will share resource to some extent between their various branches. This sharing of resource serves to achieve economies of scale. It also serves to promote a necessary controlling mechanism across the group, otherwise such groups will always tend to suffer from centrifugal forces. Each company as a matter of law will have its own directors, who will be responsible for and have a duty of care to the company of which they are directors rather than to the group of which the company is a member. Yes, it can be argued that such a director will know on which side his bread is buttered and will think very carefully before countermanding the wishes of a group director, but when the really difficult decisions are there to be taken – which is when governance is always tested most thoroughly – the director of a subsidiary will need to remember the scope of his particular responsibilities.

Groups can decide the extent to which they decentralise management responsibility. Some groups will favour centralisation. They will have group support functions, such as HR, finance, marketing and IT, which will then be deployed across the local business units. Other groups will push resource management away from the centre to the local businesses, with only a light hand of coordination from the centre. A group that centralises resource will usually save costs, avoiding unnecessary duplication of roles from one business to another. On the other hand, a group that decentralises resource will argue that it is likely to be more responsive to local nuances. This might seem more expensive to the accountants, but if it means a bigger, better business that clients and customers respond to more enthusiastically, business leaders might describe it as an investment rather than a cost. Of course, a group in which resource is centralised is a group in which a chief executive is likely to have tighter personal control. A chief executive who chooses to allocate his resource across the businesses of the group will also need to accept that other people will have to take decisions on his behalf – decisions with which he might not necessarily agree in the first instance, but which he might find to be right in the longer term. They are after all likely to be taken by individuals closer to the action. As Ricardo Semler puts it, 'Employees must be free to question, to analyse, to investigate, and a company must be flexible enough to listen to the answers. Those habits are the key to longevity, growth and profit.'[105]

Sophisticated groups can and do take advantage of the inherent tension that exists between the companies and their directors in a group. One such over the years has been plastic injection moulders Nypro – a company of contradictions. Headquartered in the US, with 18,000 employees around the world in 49 locations in 16 countries and turning over more than a $1 billion in 2008, Nypro is a big business. But it is also privately owned by its employees. As a private corporation in the US it is under no obligation to comply with many of the governance regulations applicable to US listed companies. Notwithstanding minimal reporting requirements, Nypro prides itself on being a leader in corporate openness and transparency. Nypro publishes an annual report, audited by a major auditing firm as a matter of choice. Unusually, Nypro has separated the role of chairman and chief executive.

Nypro is also unusual in the way in which it approaches the structuring of local management. Regional businesses are directed by a board of directors comprised of senior staff drawn from other businesses in the organisation. This fosters a sense of cooperation between businesses across the organisation. Remuneration strategies also encourage cooperation. Performance-related remuneration payouts are determined by the performance of the team not the individual. Project teams also include client representatives, thus ensuring client interests are recognised. At the same time, Nypro has a strongly competitive streak. Teams and businesses compete with each other. The organisation's strong flair for innovation is driven in part by the competitive culture. Of course, the obsession with client service plays a role as well. As does the fact that good ideas developed in one part of the business will quickly find their way across the business, not because of command and control, but because of the determination to be best and the fact that senior managers find themselves responsible for several teams, if not several companies within the organisation. Indeed, Nypro's culture is a curious balance between cooperation and competition, a balance that is supported by the way it deploys its governance levers.

Institutionalising disagreement

There is another important aspect of structures that needs to be explored in the context of governance. Yes, for many, governance is about compliance and discipline; but governance failures have also shown the importance of ensuring management is challenged. Good governance is also about the ability to tell management what they do not want or choose not to hear. It is easy to see how challenges might come from independent outsiders such as non-executives or representatives of other stakeholder groups; but the best-informed individuals will always be insiders; and an important form of challenge to management will always come from inside.

Good governance should be wary of the tendency of all human beings to look for evidence to defend their own points of view, even if this risks turning blind eyes to evidence that suggests alternative options that might be better. The more serious the decisions the more important it is that challenge is institutionalised. Good decision-taking processes therefore will find room for identifying and evaluating as many alternative courses of action as possible. Organisations that are aware of the pitfalls inherent in decision-taking processes will know who the most important decision takers are, but will also be aware of their particular predilections and biases, and how these relate to previous experience, and will be on the lookout for these tainting decision taking in the present. Such organisations will find room for proper debate, forcing an examination of the contrary point of view, even if no one in the room instinctively supports it. Above all, such organisations will institutionalise and repeatedly invigorate the checks and balances, the tensions between executives and non-executives, between staff and management, and between stakeholders, which will ultimately serve as the best protection against decisions that are wilful or just wrong.

It has to be accepted, however, that internal challenge – perhaps better described as 'tolerated disobedience' – is a lot more difficult to deliver and accept than an alternative point of view delivered by an outsider. This is because of the mismatch of power. An unpopular insider has a lot more to lose than an unpopular outsider. The higher the stakes the greater the difficulty. Employment legislation might seek to protect the rights of the whistle-blower, but when your livelihood is at stake, as is your reputation for being a 'team player' in the eyes of a potential future employer, the role of whistle-blower is never an easy one to take on. It is hardly surprising therefore that when governance fails, the whistle-blower often tends to make the greatest impact after the event by saying 'I told you so' rather than during the event itself so as to prevent it happening in the first place. The former head of regulatory risk at HBOS claimed he was sacked in 2004 and effectively silenced for warning that the bank's lending policy had become dangerously risky. His claims made good press in 2009, but had little impact at the time they mattered most. Sherron Watkins, an accountant at Enron, first made her concerns known in 1996, five years before Enron collapsed. But it was not until she sent an anonymous memo to Kenneth Lay in 2001 warning that the firm 'could implode in a wave of accounting scandals' that her comments began to have an effect. And it was arguably as star witness for the prosecution after the bankruptcy that she had the greatest impact.

Whistle-blowers have a role to play in governance, and structures should make room for them, but lone individuals with important things to say are never going to be as important in a governance system as a culture that facilitates challenge to the executives. It is a question of balance, of course. Too much discipline and control and the challenge will not be made. Too little and the business will descend into anarchy. At both ends of the scale governance will fail. Unfortunately the right place in the middle is difficult to find and impossible to define.

Related to the important matter of institutionalising challenge is the equally important matter of segregating responsibilities so as to safeguard against conflicts of interest. At the heart of the scandal enveloping the House of Commons about MPs' expenses – indeed their remuneration in general – is the fact that MPs have been in effect able to vote themselves pay rises, and to approve or disapprove as suited them their own expenses policies. At the heart of any governance structure must be mechanisms for ensuring that individuals, particularly individuals charged with responsibility for other people's money, are not in a position to spend it on themselves without being obliged to obtain the sanction of another individual. Segregation of duties takes the matter a step further: one person drafts his expense form, someone else approves it, a third person needs to write the cheque. Appropriate segregation of duties is at the heart of any payroll system. It is also one of the qualities of a robust management system that auditors will look for. Segregation of duties and whistle-blowing are two facets of the same thing. Whistle-blowing will make good copy in the press, but appropriately segregating duties and responsibilities will have a greater impact, and for longer.

Structures for boards and board committees

A cornerstone of corporate governance in the UK is the 'unitary board' where all directors – executive and non-executive – in effect have the same ultimate responsibility for the business. In Continental Europe it has been more common for the directors' functions to be split between a high-level supervisory board led by the chairman and a management or executive board led by the chief executive, where the management board is responsible for day-to-day management while the supervisory board has responsibility for hiring, firing, remuneration policy and overall supervision of the management board.

The unitary structure encourages consensus around the boardroom table. On the other hand, the two-tier board structure institutionalises the sorts of checks and balances that are often argued to be at the heart of much good governance. Supervisory boards also provide opportunities for different and varied stakeholder groups to be represented round the table. Additionally, arithmeticians might argue that, as a consequence of ensuring that sufficient expertise is marshalled around the boardroom table, the unitary board might be tempted to grow too large to be effective. Boards that are too big become sounding boards rather than debating, discussion and decision-taking chambers. On 6 February 2009 RBS announced the resignation of seven non-executive directors. The disastrous performance of the bank over the previous 24 months of course meant that it was inevitable that directors would go. The seven non-execs followed both the chairman and the chief executive, but a spokesman for the bank added that a board with fewer directors would be 'better able to engage effectively in the restructuring process'.

In March 2009 Sir Richard Greenbury threw a hand grenade into governance circles by announcing a change of opinion on his part: no longer was he an advocate of the unitary board. His recent experience as a member of the board of the Dutch company Philips had convinced him of the value of Continental Europe's two-tier board structure. Greenbury went further: he contended that there was a 'good chance' that the RBS disaster would not have happened had Sir Fred Goodwin dealt with a senior board of non-executive directors. The top 20 or so companies in the UK, Greenbury argued, should move to the two-tier system. Greenbury's CV includes a spell as chairman of Marks & Spencer, and he also played a pivotal role in the changes to governance that took place in the 1990s and the early years of this century; his views are thus particularly influential.

Two-tier board structures already exist in the UK in some sectors. Sophisticated family businesses and complicated, multi-shareholder private businesses often use versions of the two-tier structure to help govern the shareholders' relationship with the business. Family interests and shareholder seats are generally kept to a higher board, often through a holding company vehicle, allowing professional managers to manage the business – unfettered except with regard to key, reserved powers relating to decisions of strategic importance.

Large charities and not-for-profits also take advantage of the two-tier structure. The board of trustees or governors (often volunteers) is in effect the board of directors. But the day-to-day management of the organisation itself is left to a management team of salaried employees led by a chief executive, who may or may not have the right to attend trustee meetings.

It is important to recognise that the role of director in a company with a two-tier board will differ from the role of director in a firm with a unitary board. I have worked with several companies with two-tier boards that have had problems appreciating the difference. It might be thought that separating out the supervisory board from the executive board should have the effect of clarifying the distinction between non-executive and executive, but in my experience this is not necessarily true. Supervisory board members occasionally get frustrated at their lack of ability to wrestle with and influence executive matters. They can suffer from a sense of being 'managed' by the executives, who, even if indirectly, influence the content of the supervisory board's agenda. Unless the executives and non-executives are gathered around the same table it can be difficult for the non-executives to understand what is going on. On the other hand, executives have expressed frustration that the supervisory board has slowed down necessary decisions and has attempted to step beyond its supervisory remit into an executive capacity. It can be understood why executives suffering from this syndrome might be tempted to 'manage' the supervisory board to whom they report, just in the interests of getting things done. Undoubtedly, splitting the board adds a layer of complexity. If things go well a two-tier board has the potential to add real and significant value to decision taking. Because of the added complexity there are also more reasons why things might go wrong. As always in governance there are no easy answers.

In practice, many companies in the UK with unitary boards have in effect a form of multi-layer board structure, created not by a supervisory board / management board split, or by the use of holding companies, but through the use of board committees. Big businesses will commonly have an audit committee to monitor the integrity of financial reporting and to supervise relations with auditors, internal and external, and a remuneration committee to consider the remuneration of the directors. An appointments or nominations committee to handle appointments to the board and other senior posts is not unusual. Companies will have other board committees too.

Board committees help focus the attention of directors with specialist skills on specialist items. They also provide opportunities for advisers and other non-board members to contribute to the debate, thus adding to the number of individuals influencing the direction of the company, without turning the boardroom itself into a conference centre. Board committees are committees of the board. A decision taken by a board committee is a decision taken on behalf of the board as a whole, and thus most key committee decisions will need to be taken to the board itself for further consideration and ratification. But a committee will not have done its job if, as a consequence, the amount of time devoted to the topic by the main board is not significantly reduced.

That board committees have become an integral part of the governance regime is demonstrated by the fact that they receive their own attention in the Combined Code. Although all of the committees mentioned above receive some coverage in the Combined Code, the Financial Reporting Council has gone on to pay special attention to the role of the audit committee and has published guidance (the third edition in October 2008) running to 26 pages just on its own. The audit committee of a company subject to the Combined Code should be comprised of independent non-executive directors. The chairman of the company may in certain circumstances be a member of the committee, but only if he is himself independent, and only if he is not the chair of the committee. The committee is expected to meet auditors, internal and external, without management being present. The relation between the committee and the board itself is the subject of specific comment:

> Nothing in the guidance should be interpreted as a departure from the principle of the unitary board. All directors remain equally responsible for the company's affairs as a matter of law. The audit committee, like other committees to which particular responsibilities are delegated (such as the remuneration committee), remains a committee of the board. Any disagreement within the board, including disagreement between the audit committee's members and the rest of the board, should be resolved at board level.[106]

Perhaps more interesting still are comments in the introductory pages about the nature of governance itself:

> ... the most important features of this relationship cannot be drafted as guidance or put into a code of practice: a frank, open working relationship and a high level of mutual respect are essential, particularly between the audit committee chairman and the board chairman, the chief executive and the finance director. The audit committee must be prepared to take a robust stand, and all parties must be prepared to make information freely available to the audit committee, to listen to their views and to talk through the issues openly.[107]

Even codes themselves are now recognising that governance needs to be more than a series of codes, and the behaviour expected of managers (and indeed other stakeholders) more than a matter of simple compliance with them.

Structures in family businesses

As has already been noted, family businesses have taken governance seriously for longer than most organisations and authorities. Family businesses unsurprisingly have adopted their own distinctive structures. There are no templates for family businesses. Family governance architecture and its linking communication mechanisms need to be custom-designed to match every family's unique requirements.

Family businesses often lend themselves to versions of the 'two-tier' or 'dual' board types of structure that are relatively rare in corporate UK but common in Continental Europe. The separation of the main board from the operations board can take several forms. In some family businesses the 'main board' is actually the board of a holdings company, whereas the 'operations board' is the board of a subsidiary. Other companies might have the same boards gathered into the same company.

Multi-generational family businesses can be diversified into a number of separate business units or divisions (often managed by a mix of cousins and non-family professional managers), which are controlled by an operations board (sometimes called a trading board). An elaborate governance structure in turn supervises the operations board, including via a main board (sometimes called a holdings or supervisory board) with representatives from family branches plus outside directors, along with a family council and family assembly.

In many large family businesses the main forum through which the distinctive interests and concerns of family members and shareholders can be communicated is the family council. At its best, a family council in a multi-generational business probably has up to 10 elected members representing all family members, generations and branches. It is a working group serving as an 'executive' committee of the family assembly. The family council will operate as a bridge between the board of directors of the family business and the family shareholders.

In family businesses, the board of directors has an extra area of responsibility beyond those of non-family enterprises. Board members must understand the family's relationship with the company, mediate its influence on the business and help ensure that the family's reasonable long-term goals for the business are met. Money may not be the family's only, or even a significant driver. A key function of the family council is to send clear signals to the board of directors on these 'strategic', long-term issues – for example, business risk and reward parameters that are acceptable to the family, the return on investment sought by family shareholders, and the family's attitude to ethical and moral issues that may arise in connection with business operations. As the family expands and becomes more detached from the business, the family council often switches its focus to communication, social, educational and charitable issues, reserving these strategic policy decisions to an executive family team.

The family council, which may include family managers as well as family owners, should operate on a consensus basis, not by majority vote or in accordance with shareholding. (Indeed, it is a general rule for all these family governance structures that voting is to be avoided, except as a last resort.) The council has no formal business authority, but it aims to create the family 'glue', enabling the family to speak with one voice to the board. In fact, family shareholders can be seen as having just one role – to back the board of directors: if they are unable to provide this backing, then they have the ultimate power to remove that board. For smaller families, the council might well comprise all the family shareholders, but for complex cousin-owned businesses that have large numbers of family shareholders, traditionally each branch of the family has tended to nominate someone for election to the family council. Recent trends, however, suggest that families are trying to move away from the notion of branch representation, often seen as a potentially divisive concept. Currently, in some more mature UK family businesses, the new generation has been adopting fresh guidelines that use instead policies and procedures designed to emphasise and foster a more unified family approach to the business – clearly a development that places a high premium on establishing and maintaining good intra-family communication.

In large families there needs to be an open forum for all family shareholders or all family members from the different branches of the family to meet and discuss family issues and concerns relating to the business, and to learn and ask questions about its activities. Many families call this the family assembly. Assembly meetings should be scheduled to maximise attendance, and are often combined with social activities. They provide an opportunity for accountability, with family leaders who work in the family governance process able to report back to the wider family. Family assemblies should also aim to teach family members about the business through presentations, and to discuss in broad terms the direction the company is taking and how this might change in the future. They can also announce any changes in share ownership since the last meeting, and possible regulatory or tax changes that might have an impact on the family. Families need to decide at what age children should attend these meetings. Whatever the age limit – if there is one – families should organise group activities so that the next generation can learn about the business and develop relationships with their siblings and cousins.

As well as family councils and assemblies, the family governance architecture in many Middle Eastern family businesses includes an extra body – a council of elders or seniors. Because of deep-seated respect for the senior generation that underpins many aspects of Middle Eastern life and culture, this entity will be at the top of the family governance hierarchy, with the family council acting as its executive committee.

Other family businesses also have a 'family office', responsible for centralising functions for family members and, by acting as an investment, liquidity management and administrative centre, helping underpin the family governance structure. It can also oversee family estate and tax planning, and coordinate insurance, banking and accounting. Many families believe stronger family ties will develop for future generations when a dedicated office exists, because it helps foster a strong family identity, clarifies family values, preserves traditions and trains young people to responsibly manage the money they will one day inherit. Another useful function of a family office is to administer a family fund (often financed by a set percentage of dividend payouts) set up to cover specific agreed items of family expenditure on behalf of family members. Such a fund can seek to maintain financial equality among family branches, which may be unbalanced by factors such as unequal numbers of children in the next generation or a medical emergency. The family fund covers specific items of expenditure considered to be a family rather than an individual responsibility, such as for education, medical expenses, share buy-back loans, the refinancing of shares for future generations and family venture capital.

The family office is a separate operation from the family business, although some of the same individuals may participate in both. It should have a formal business structure with a management board (which can consist of family members as well as outside advisers) and it should report to the family on investment performance, liquidity and other operating information. Through planning together, a family can create a shared vision and an articulation of principles and guidelines that will help direct overall investment policies. In addition, combining assets into investment pools can increase buying power and provide access to better money managers. A central value-added service of family office operations should also support independence – the provision of unbiased, non-product-motivated advice on asset allocation and diversification – while the determination of an appropriate asset allocation and investment management strategy takes place with a comprehensive understanding of the family's financial situation and its risk–return objectives.

There are two main family office models – the single-family office (SFO) and multi-family office (MFO). The SFO is the traditional model, serving a single family, but SFOs are tending to die out. Rising costs and the difficulty of retaining top-quality talent are causing fewer families to open individual offices. MFOs, which offer services to more than one family, are often formed by a family deciding to open the doors of its SFO to other families. This has the advantage of providing the career structure, challenge and motivation for talented people that the SFO may not, of spreading costs and risks across a larger asset base, and the opportunity to establish the MFO as a sustainable business. While family offices have traditionally operated around the investment component of wealth management, today they are addressing broader aspects of family wealth. In particular, there is greater emphasis being placed on human, intellectual and social capital perspectives, and more concern about the ways in which family wealth affects the lives of heirs. Consequently, many family offices are focusing on the need to create educational programmes for the next generation, giving them the skills required to make independent evaluations regarding the family's wealth. The expertise of the family office can be put to good use in educating the next generation from an early age about the challenges and responsibilities of wealth, investment and philanthropy – and in offering opportunities to gain hands-on experience of dealing with those responsibilities.

Board behaviour

As is now only too evident, at the heart of any governance system – whether for listed or private company, partnership, limited company, family business, for-profit or not-for-profit – is the board. Who sits on the board, and their qualifications and experience, are critical; as are the mechanisms designed to incentivise them. The structure of the board also has a key influence – the balance between executive and non-executive, the role of committees and the formal roles assigned to individuals around the boardroom table. But perhaps most important of all is the behaviour of the board itself, and how it approaches its duties and responsibilities. This is a function of the way all of the issues and elements discussed so far in this book interact. Some conclusions can be drawn about good boards from the previous discussion, and at the risk of repetition, are worth restating here.

Good boards debate

Yes, directors do have a role as sounding boards, but directors should be wary of any tendency on their part to act merely as sounding boards. The sounding-board function is best discharged by directors as individuals. When acting collectively as a board, directors need to debate – which means actively engage and wrestle with the issues that matter.

Good boards challenge

A good board therefore will not be packed with people primed to agree with the executives. A board that challenges needs people with qualifications, experience and guts. A good board will see challenge as a good thing, not a time-consuming obstruction.

Good boards manage conflicts of interest

Boards must be aware of their own inherent conflicts of interest, expose them and do their best to cope with them. Structure and process can weaken potential conflicts of interest, but cannot eliminate them altogether. Individuals will always be prejudiced in favour of their own ideas. 'Executive directors,' as Sir Adrian Cadbury observes, 'are on both sides of the divide ... between direction and management,'[108] and thus immediately conflicted when they enter the boardroom. Many ambitious people would rather get on with doing than sit around talking about it. Good boards acknowledge these conflicts of interest and look out for times when they threaten the quality of decision taking.

Good boards initiate

An entity's strategy is the responsibility of the board. Yes, it is only to be expected that the CEO will take a leading role in shaping the future direction of the company, but it is more likely that the future of the company will be safeguarded when it is recognised that the responsibility for that direction is the board's not the CEO's. The best test of this is a board that recognises its role in initiating strategy rather than merely rubber-stamping someone else's.

Good boards decide

Too many boards suffer from the delusion that they are deciding, when in reality it is the executives who do the deciding. It has been observed that juries in court cases tend to fall into two types: evidence-based and verdict-based juries. Evidence-based juries usually do not take a vote until after assessing the evidence. Jury members say what they think before taking a decision. Verdict-based juries on the other hand vote first, then do the discussing afterwards. Verdict-based juries therefore are inclined to spend time eliminating the dissenters, rather than spend time improving the quality of the decision. Boards can fall into the same trap. Boards that appreciate their role as decision takers will force themselves to behave otherwise – and executives and chairman who appreciate the importance of this will ensure they do so.

Good boards review their own performance

The most important objective of governance is to ensure that the right decisions are made in the first place. But the second most important objective has to be to ensure that the right decisions will be made next time too. Good boards will have formal mechanisms for reviewing the performance not just of individual directors but of the board as a group.

Good boards refresh and revitalise themselves

Good boards recognise the need for fresh thinking. The easiest way of enshrining all of the other good board behaviours is to ensure that no director sees his or her appointment as a job for life, or, conversely, sees perpetual reappointment as the only indicator of personal success. Similarly, good boards recognise that there is no one ideal structure but several, and change from one to another in and of itself will help foster the process of renewal. Lastly, good boards recognise that revitalisation, combined with review, are the most powerful ways of ensuring that good board performance is sustained.

Meetings

For many management teams, sorting out the discipline of management meetings is a key issue in improving business performance. It is also a key component of good governance.

In big businesses board discipline is a function of the role of the chairman. But in smaller businesses, where the roles are less likely to be defined, and the functioning of the board itself will on occasions be difficult to separate from the functioning of the management team, the pragmatics of execution as opposed to the disciplines of governance are down to the founding entrepreneur or the managing director, and what applies to board meetings applies to all senior management meetings. It is, however, too easy to assume that meetings in big companies are disciplined and well run, and meetings in small businesses are not. What constitutes an effective management meeting will differ from business to business, but there are some characteristics that are worth noting.

Formality and frequency

Just ensuring disciplined meetings are held is a good start. Entrepreneurial businesses exist for far too long without properly structuring meetings and decision-taking processes. Once these meetings and processes have been created they have got to be worked at. Too many work hard at creating structures, but still allow the big decisions to be taken informally. Regardless of when the board meets as a board, the management team needs to meet as a management team formally about once a week. The key word here is 'formally'. In young businesses the management team is probably meeting informally all the time, but this is not a substitute for the process of a formal, structured meeting. In bigger businesses, informality is rarely sufficient; if formal structures have not been created to compensate for the declining influence of informal structures, decision taking will fall into a vacuum.

Reporting

Disciplined reporting involves reviewing the present and the past. This requires members of the senior management team to report on ongoing business. Many business teams find it useful for team members to commit their reports to paper and distribute their reports ahead of the meeting. It is the responsibility of all to prepare themselves by reading paperwork ahead of the meeting – but it is an unwise chairman or managing director who relies on this alone to identify issues worthy of attention. Team members should take it in turn to comment on their own reports and then take questions and comments from the others in the meeting itself.

Anticipating and planning

In addition to reviewing the past and the present, the team needs to discuss the future. Inevitably future issues will be raised when reviewing the present and the past, but this mechanism is insufficient for identifying future issues. The managing director should ensure that the team is organised to anticipate and structure responses to future developments. The right word for this sort of activity is 'planning'. Notes on the annual planning cycle are outside the scope of this book, but it is in the interests of good governance in any business, large or small, that there is a formal planning process; and though the process will be steered by the board or the senior management team, it will work best if it takes place outside the normal structure of board meetings. Planning for the future demands different styles of thinking from reporting and reviewing; it needs a different style of meeting.

Meeting efficiency

One of the reasons that many business people get impatient with meetings is that too many take too long to discuss the blindingly obvious – indeed many meetings are characterised by interminable discussions, with boredom being the only reason for passing from one agenda item to another. I take my clients through a process I call 'twice round the table'. Each agenda item is introduced by an individual. Once the team is satisfied that they understand the issue that is being tabled, each member of the team then takes it in turn to comment – uninterrupted – on the issue, to raise concerns and to question. Once everyone has had their say, the individual responsible for the item will then summarise, and restate the issue as revised by the discussion, and if needed table a draft conclusion or decision. Each individual in the team will then be offered the opportunity to comment again on the issue – but only if he or she has a new comment to bring to the table. The managing director will close the agenda item with the resolution of the issue. This sort of process is an effective way of improving meeting efficiency. Behind it is the premise that most discussions in most meetings go round and round in circles if the discussion is undisciplined, and anything more than two rounds of discussion will not yield much value. In addition, some individuals will dominate the discussion unnecessarily and others will fail to give value by being too quiet. Many governance failures start here. This sort of discipline can help both these problems. It will make it more likely that a decision will be taken and that the decision taken will be a good one.

Documentation

Meetings need documenting. Agendas circulated in advance together with discussion papers are helpful. Minutes that at least record the decisions taken are critical. Decisions also need taking about who has access to minutes. Small businesses often exist without either agendas or minutes. Big businesses have both. Turning from one type of business into the other is one of the changes that happen when businesses grow – and grow up.

12 | Straight thinking about the future

> 'Things fall apart; the centre cannot hold;
> Mere anarchy is loosed upon the world,
> The blood-dimmed tide is loosed, and everywhere
> The ceremony of innocence is drowned;
> The best lack all conviction, while the worst
> Are full of passionate intensity.'
>
> W. B. Yeats, 'The Second Coming'

'The key issue to keep in mind,' wrote Adrian Cadbury in 2002, 'is that the nature of the boundaries within which companies operate is continually changing.'[109] Never has this been more true than in 2009, as I tidy up this book for the publisher, when the world seems to be falling apart. Monsters not seen since the 1930s are haunting the streets, and worrying those hurrying every day to work – those lucky enough to have work, that is. There is a sense that the centre is indeed struggling to hold firm. The worst have already shown signs of a passionate intensity, while those who are trying to reflect steadily on the best way forward seem unsure how to act, and certainly seem to lack conviction. The traditional levers for sorting out the corporate world have been pulled, but so far seem to have had little effect, and policy makers are reaching beyond the known for solutions that are as yet untried, and seem (if the markets are any indicators) to stand an equal chance of making matters worse rather than better. Indeed, policy makers have been part of the problem. MPs, after weeks of obfuscation, followed by days of denial and repeated claims of 'I've done nothing wrong,' and 'I've not broken any rules,' set about climbing over each other to talk to camera about their values and the amount of expenses they have volunteered to pay back to the taxpayer, and then started resigning, or at least indicating their intention not to stand at the next election.

Learning lessons

As far as the economic crisis is concerned, we have been here before, and many times. Indeed, the most surprising thing about the current economic crisis is the fact that it has taken us by surprise. The economy since time immemorial has surged forward and backwards. It takes someone as smart as a prime minister or a chancellor of the exchequer to believe that boom and bust has been abolished, and then to put the country's money where his faith is. History has taught us before that it is only a question of time before such a faith is found wanting. If so many of our best and most influential economic thinkers could be fooled into thinking 'this time it is different', the rest of us can perhaps be forgiven. But history also tells us that even when times are bad there are still opportunities to take. Analysis by Merrill Lynch shows that during the last six recessions alcohol, tobacco and casino stocks have, on average, returned 11 per cent against a 1.5 per cent loss for the S&P 500. These stocks actually increased absolute earnings in each of these recessions as well. And there are other, less sinful sources of opportunity in a downturn: consumers will still go on holiday, but closer to home, and for less time; people will still look for treats, but smaller ones; people who have paid for, or who have yet to pay for, their children will be more likely to spend on extras than those still paying – who in turn will still prioritise family and education. Bad times throw up brand-new sources of opportunity too. Many big businesses will give up on good opportunities as well as bad ones when cash is tight – to someone else's advantage. And there are all those businesses structured to deliver when times are good that will need re-engineering for different times, thus presenting opportunities to some – think of all those lean, just-in-time supply chains only one bankruptcy away from collapse.

Times of economic uncertainty also present opportunities for those interested in reworking governance. The turmoil that followed the dot.com crash and the scandals surrounding Enron, WorldCom, Tyco and so on led to significant reviews of the governance frameworks. The Cadbury Report, *Financial Aspects of Corporate Governance*, published in 1992, was triggered by the failures of BCCI, Polly Peck and Maxwell Communications. Earlier still, and perhaps more pertinently for 2009, the raft of regulation introduced by F.D. Roosevelt as part of the New Deal was a consequence of the Great Depression, the start of which was signalled by (though not necessarily caused by) the Wall Street Crash of 1929. The economic crisis that started to surface in 2007, gathered steam in 2008 and started to unleash its full fury in 2009 presents another such opportunity to rethink governance. Where will this next opportunity for soul-searching take us?

Many of the themes that currently engage thinkers about governance have already been referred to in this book. But it is worth drawing some of them together as we attempt to make sense of the often conflicting proposals for solving the crisis we currently find ourselves in. Inevitably when discussing governance issues we have looked backwards, but only accountants (and bad ones at that) are interested in what has happened: real managers are interested in the decisions they have to take now and next year. As we draw our themes together, are there lessons we can learn that will help us govern our businesses better in the future?

The first thing I note is to repeat that we have been here before: indeed we are here after every financial crisis, except that each time the chorus of disapproval gets more strident and the calls for reform more shrill. Several conclusions might be drawn from this: one might be, with due respect to George Santayana, that we are condemned to repeat the lessons of history because we never learn from them. As has been noted, the history of regulation of the banking industry since 1929 has broadly been a timeline traced from a period of little regulation through a period of lots of regulation, to the last 15 years, a period when regulation has been gradually unpicked again by legislators who are not old enough to have lived through the crisis that led to the regulation in the first place. As I write, one of the consequences of the crisis of 2009 seems inevitably the re-regulating of what had already once been regulated in the first place.

Perhaps another lesson of history is that no governance regime will ever be strong enough to keep the lid on the kettle of a boom. When people throng together and pull in one direction, is it ever possible to stand against them and survive? Heroes that fought successfully against evil forces always were semi-divine, and were, unfortunately, therefore mythological. Managers are only made of flesh and blood, and stand little chance against the forces of history. As Charles Mackay wrote in 1852, 'Men, it has been well said, think in herds; it will be seen that they go mad in herds.'[110]

Perhaps, alternatively, from our review of history we have to draw the conclusion that much of our thinking about governance to date has just been misguided, and that if we are to make governance work we have to explore new approaches. We do not need to look for those who have broken rules or ignored guidance. Although there have been and always will be some companies that wilfully ignore the rules and who treat guidance no more seriously than smokers treat government health warnings, we need to remember that RBS complied with the Combined Code; and even Enron up to a few weeks before its demise was extolled as a shining example of corporate governance. If so, the challenge is to find new ways of understanding governance, and to ensure companies apply it in ways that last – at least through the next boom and into the inevitable bust that lies beyond it, and which, we may hope, will be less traumatic than the one that governance yet again failed to ameliorate in the years running up to 2009.

The second thing I note is that, though we have been here before, the world this time around is undoubtedly a more complicated place than it was last time. And next time, it is fair to predict, it will be more complicated again. For businesses big and small a lot of this has to do with globalisation, and even if an unfortunate consequence of the current crisis is that the barriers will go up and international trade will suffer, the world will still be left a more interconnected place than it was before, with businesses sitting across international borders and economic fault lines. Even small firms find themselves at the centre of international supply chains of a complexity that would have been impossible to imagine just one recession ago.

International complexities are exacerbated by technological complexities. In recent years technology has not just transformed communication, it has transformed relations between people. Technology has brought people closer together, and driven them further apart. After exchanging emails with a colleague on a different continent, a director might prefer to email a colleague at the next desk rather than turn and talk to him. In many lines of business, particularly in the City, decisions are no longer taken by individuals at all, but by computers, assessing the odds, reacting to pre-programmed trigger points and then exercising their algorithms. In such circumstances governance is hard pressed to keep up, particularly when we recall the importance of face-to-face communication in governance, and the role communication plays in challenge, debate, check and balance.

Thirdly, and perhaps a further manifestation of the complexity just referred to, the distinctions that helpfully used to keep sectors and segments of the commercial world discrete are blurring. Banks design and sell 'products'. Car manufacturers sell finance packages. Social enterprises are led by social entrepreneurs. Listed companies need the flexibility of small businesses otherwise they will miss the opportunities that matter. In the virtual world, a small business can seem as big as a big one. Is an investor in convertibles holding debt or equity? Or debt masquerading as equity? Companies set up shop on Second Life, a virtual world where you can exist, if you wish, as your own avatar, with an attitude to business at several removes from the one you adopt in the office. Governance is always easier when organisations, as well as people, keep to their allotted places in the scheme of things and respect the boundaries that regulators have imagined for them. The tidy world that Frederick Taylor described, in which people knew their tasks and did them, in which companies existed for the benefit of shareholders, and in which the only sin was to not make a profit, has morphed into something far less tidy. Governance's attempts to keep up with the pace of change and the disintegration of the old order have spawned codes for different corners of the economy, and have resulted in oscillations between regulation and principle and deregulation and back again, but one is left with a nagging feeling that governance is always on the back foot, or struggling just to keep in touch.

Fourthly, it is possible to detect a change in the nature

of the relation between the individual and the workplace as represented by the organisational hierarchy and the rulebook. I've already quoted Charles Mackay observing that men go mad in herds. He goes on to say that 'they only recover their senses slowly, and one by one.'[111] Management is a collective act, of course, and much in governance addresses how people relate to each other and how they act in groups. But for governance to work at all organisations depend on the personal attitude of individuals to their own responsibilities. The relation of individuals to their organisations is changing. Staff are less respectful of their superiors than of old. They have less patience with hierarchies. They want to get to the top quicker. They do not engage with the printed word as much as their older colleagues. Increasingly, the organisational cultures that are finding favour and success reflect these changes; they are creative, chaotic cultures, and the structures that foster them are fluid, flat, flexible structures. In the interests of efficiency, controls and roles that do not add value to the process or the quality of the decision ('redundancies', as the theorists call them) are being stripped out. These changing sociological qualities and characteristics present challenges to those looking to governance mechanisms to help them run their businesses. The continuing failures of governance suggest that so far, by and large, approaches to governance have not quite risen to the challenge.

A personal responsibility

Like bonus schemes, governance regimes are only too often designed by those that like them for the benefit of those who, at best, are indifferent to them, or who see them as a necessary evil. Change management only works at the level of the individual, otherwise it is an abstraction, or a futile act of flag waving. Governance is the same; governance has to engage with people at the level of the individual if it is to be taken seriously, otherwise it will turn into what it is, in effect, for too many to start off with – a process of ticking boxes; an exercise in compliance; a cost of doing business rather than something that adds value; an empty ceremony. This has to change if organisations and the people in them are going to address successfully the challenges that the 21st century is presenting. Governance has to become something people want, rather than something they just complain about, comply with or put up with.

There is another side to this proposition – that managers have to acknowledge that governance will work best in the new world if they accept that the most important elements in any governance mechanism are those that rely on their own personal contributions as individuals, on personal responsibility and on trust. This sort of thinking is not new. James Surowiecki writes in his fascinating book *The Wisdom of Crowds* about the influence of Quakerism in the development of industry in 18th- and early 19th-century England. Quakers owned half of the county's ironworks. They founded Barclays and Lloyds. Much of the confectionery industry was in Quaker hands, as was the transatlantic trade. Quakers were so influential in business because of their reputation for honesty – an honesty that generated prosperity. Trust has always been at the heart of well-ordered capitalism. Daniel Defoe described an honest tradesman as 'a jewel indeed, and valued wherever he is found'. As Surowiecki writes, 'Over centuries ... the evolution of capitalism has been in the direction of more trust and transparency.'[112] Trust and responsibility continue to be qualities on which commerce depends. When the queues formed outside branches of Northern Rock in early 2008 it was evident that it was not just the bank that was in trouble, but the fundamental underpinnings of the economic system.

Of course, trust and responsibility are recognised as key components in any governance framework. But the actions of many seem to demonstrate, and many of the codes seem to presume, that trust and responsibility are things that cannot be left to managers, but need institutionalising and codifying before they count. In so doing, trust and responsibility, in the forms they take in corporate governance become not the things themselves, but pale imitations, from which individuals seem to be able to dissociate at will, and to which too many seem only too content to pay lip service. The presumption has been that individuals when left to their own devices will allow ambition to morph into greed, and business stewardship into an opportunity for furthering self-interest. Look no lower than the House of Commons if you want some evidence. Governance itself looks once again like just an empty ceremony.

At the heart of effective governance in the future, therefore, has to be a new conception of the role of the manager. Alternative visions are already being developed for the next generation of manager. In February 2009 Gary Hamel, London Business School professor and business guru, set out in an article a new programme of inquiry for business thinkers and a new set of challenges for managers. Many of his proposed challenges touch on themes we have discussed: 'Eliminate the pathologies of formal hierarchy,' 'Reduce fear and increase trust,' 'Redefine the work of leadership,' 'Develop holistic performance measures.'[113] Others of his challenges cut to the quick of modern governance:

> Ensure that the work of management serves a higher
> purpose. Most companies strive to maximise shareholder
> wealth – a goal that is inadequate in many respects.
> As an emotional catalyst, wealth maximisation lacks
> the power to fully mobilise human energies. It is an

insufficient defence when people question the legitimacy
of corporate power. And it is not specific or compelling
enough to spur renewal. For these reasons, tomorrow's
management practices must focus on the achievement of
socially significant and noble goals. [114]

Hamel's propositions, though striking, are not new.
Indeed they have been around since the founding fathers of
capitalism. Adam Smith's first book was not *The Wealth of
Nations,* often cited as the bible of free market economics,
but *The Theory of Moral Sentiments,* in which he argues that
while 'prudence' is 'of all virtues that which is most helpful to
the individual', it is 'humanity, justice, generosity, and public
spirit,' that are 'the qualities most useful to others.' [115]

Am I advocating that we take down our frameworks and
throw away our codes? Of course not. Such a strategy would
be naïve. Codes and frameworks can usefully set standards
and manage expectations and provide an architecture in
which trust and responsibility can thrive. To a lesser extent,
frameworks can also ensure that those who are determined
not to follow the standard are duly identified and dealt with
– though this will always only be to a lesser extent. But it has
become incontrovertibly evident, I suggest, that the frameworks and codes are failing to deliver on their own. Only personal attitude and responsibility can bring them to life. As
Gandhi once observed, 'Good government is no substitute
for self-government.' MPs should take note. This demands
a significant change in our understanding of management,
what it is and the elements in it that should be admired and
held up for admiration.

Future perfect

What do these changes look like? Every individual involved in management – certainly everyone with responsibility for others, and responsibilities that affect others in different parts of their organisations and outside – needs to accept that governance will only work if we all take responsibility for bringing it to life. This includes some acceptance of change at the top of organisations. For governance to work – for businesses to work – managers need to redefine their own roles. There needs to be a recognition that with personal accountability goes a due sense of modesty. After the departure of RBS Chief Executive Sir Fred Goodwin, one of his erstwhile colleagues observed, 'He was trying to do everyone else's job ... but he wasn't doing his own job.'[116] No, most businesses never have been and never will be democracies. Difficult and unpopular decisions will still need to be taken, and it will always be true that a bad decision in many ways is better than no decision at all: if the consequence of governance is that decision taking is slowed down to the extent that decisions are not taken, then governance will have also failed us. A bad decision can be followed by a good one. The absence of a decision takes an organisation nowhere. But decision takers need to accept and appreciate the value of robust challenge and debate, and need to build into their decision-taking processes mechanisms that ensure such challenge is provided and acted on. Decision takers also need to accept that they will be wrong on occasion and will need to back down. This will undoubtedly be helped if we throw away the cult of business leader as hero. Heroes, as has already been noted, were always creatures of myth in any case. But self-styled business heroes will not be able to acquire new habits of modesty and self-restraint if left to themselves.

Part of the change of approach to management will be a further rethinking of the importance of education, training and qualification. *Accountancy* magazine reported in March 2009 that 37 of the 97 FTSE-100 audit committee chairs did not even have an accountancy qualification.[117] None of the 37 were in breach of the Combined Code, which requires only that at least one member of the audit committee has 'recent and relevant financial experience'.[118] Similarly, it is either an indictment of management and their attitude to education and qualification, or of the qualification regime itself, that so many of those holding top jobs in the banking industry have not trained professionally as bankers to the extent of being able to obtain a professional qualification in their area of supposed expertise. Perhaps it is time, however, to go even further. Perhaps there needs to be a professional training, qualifying, accreditation and post-qualifying development regime programme for board directors. That so many board directors are qualified accountants (including Sir Fred Goodwin, it should be noted) hints at the need for a more appropriate and focused qualification for those responsible for the key decisions in certainly the biggest companies in the land. If there is increasingly an expectation, if not a requirement, that an individual possess a recognised qualification before managing a professional football club, it seems not beyond the realms of reasonableness that there should be an appropriately robust management or director qualification for those deemed fit to act as directors of listed companies.

Perhaps, if boards – certainly boards of listed companies, and those other entities sat at the centre of complex networks of remote stakeholders – were comprised of individuals who were obliged to demonstrate their understanding and expertise by way of educational attainment, rather than just 'hard knocks' or 'the University of Life', we might stand a better chance of improving the quality of the individuals who have the greatest influence on governance: company directors. If a director's competence was certified, she would have to rely less on the other directorships listed on her CV to evidence her competence, and the directors' circuit would stop being a self-perpetuating ring of self-interest in which directors select each other for roles in each other's companies. An increase in the number of qualified, capable directors would lead to greater independence on the part of directors themselves, which in turn would increase the confidence of boards, making it less likely that CEOs will bulldoze through strategy that is not in their companies' long-term interests, even if it satisfies some short-term performance target.

Fewer items are more important on this agenda than a change of approach to remuneration. Regulation will help, but it is the attitude that needs to change too. Sir Fred Goodwin's reward for his tenure at RBS was retirement at 50 on an annual pension for life set initially at least at almost £700,000 (and subsequently revised downwards 'voluntarily' on Sir Fred's part to the still princely £342,500). Yes – that's the amount he is to earn *after* he stepped down from RBS. This has been described as 'falling upwards', a phenomenon that too many executives seem to have benefited from. But, if the amount that individuals earn when they retire astonishes, it pales compared to the amounts some have earned when still in charge. Individuals have been encouraged to put the pursuit of untold personal wealth as the number one personal objective. This is why, we are told, their phones are always on, and why their clients can call them at 3.00 am. It is the deal that's been done at investment banks: we take your body, you take our money. But pacts like this have been shown to be Faustian, and have encouraged a culture where greed has been a stronger motivator than satisfaction, where staff have been more excited by their bonuses than their integrity, and decisions have been taken in the interests of personal reward rather than in the interests of the company. Talk of needing to align executives with their shareholders by loading the executives with equity and options has been hypocritical. No one should be fooled: managers have ended up loving the reward, not the shareholder; and in many instances shareholder interests – indeed, all stakeholder interests – have suffered as a consequence.

It is an attitude that increasingly prevails across organisations and does not just sit in the boardroom. In *The Art of War*, Sun Tzu argues that if you have to fight a battle, make sure you fight with everything you have. Just as governance is about more than satisfying the needs of one set of stakeholders, so satisfaction, motivation and reward should be about more than remuneration. More's the pity then that too many organisations choose to fight talent wars just with money. If you want to recruit the best it is too easy to assume that you just need to pay more. If you have the best already, supposedly all you need to do to retain them is match any offer made during an enemy raid. Conversely, if you want to recruit laterally, the logic of the war-game demands that you bribe someone else's employee to sacrifice the haven that is their current organisation for the risk of joining yours. Such a mindset also diverts attention from the qualities that distinguish one organisation from another. A strategy too reliant on an influx of recruits bribed to swap sides from the enemy runs the risk of diluting the uniqueness of your proposition. Where does this leave you? Paying too much for staff who accidentally destroy the very qualities that gave you the ability to afford them in the first place. This is a battle that only the fittest (and fattest) can win in the short term. And in the long term a pay-based strategy is a zero-sum game in which even the fittest risk destroying themselves. Nowhere is doomsday seen more clearly than in public service. Capable individuals used to seek public service for many reasons, but rarely was it money. Now it is only too common for the leadership teams of public sector organisations to be stuffed with individuals

earning six-figure salaries. We are told that it is important
that the public sector competes with the private in the war
for talent. The assumption is that individuals in the public
sector need to be dragged down to the same ways of thinking that prevail in the private sector in order, not to motivate
them, but to satisfy notions of fairness. In the endgame we see
officials paid six-figure termination packages for failing, and
MPs married to each other making second-home claims for
different second homes. Yes, I suppose this satisfies a notion
of 'fairness' somewhere. And MPs continue to point out, in
their defence, apparently, that they broke no rules.

The alternative? A culture and an attitude of mind that
leads organisations to take a more holistic approach to the
value that individuals create, and through which individuals
appreciate that they get more from the organisations they
work for than money; that, as John Ruskin put it, 'there is no
wealth but life'.[119] Organisations that understand this, and
which, unfortunately, have to be described as really brave,
make sure there is a fundamental disconnect between performance and reward – a space that then must be filled by
an assessment of the value an individual really brings to the
firm. This is perhaps the only way of ensuring remuneration
and reward do not descend into a numbers-driven downward
spiral. Again, codes and regulations can have some effect here,
as does the board, but at the end of the day what is needed is
a change of attitude and mindset on the part of the employee
and the firm. As the fuss about Sir Fred Goodwin's pension
got stronger, Sir Fred wrote a letter to Treasury Minister Lord
Myners, defending his initial decision not to hand back any
of his pension fund. Sir Fred wrote:

> I am told that the topic of my pension was specifically
> raised with you by both the chairman of the group
> remuneration committee, and the group chairman, and

you indicated that you were aware of my entitlement,
and that no further 'gestures' would be required.

What is particularly disturbing to me about the pension
row – even more than the sums of money involved – is this
talk about 'gestures'. 'Gestures' take us to a mindset and an
attitude where governance and its accompanying framework
of codes and rules have a ceremonial rather than a functional
role. If we want governance to really matter it has to be taken
to a level where it is about more than 'gestures'.

Such changes are difficult to deliver. But they have been
before, and can be again. Times of crisis offer good opportunities for delivering them. With such a change of attitude,
with a bit of passionate intensity and conviction, maybe,
just maybe, we will stand a better chance this time round of
making governance work for all managers.

Acknowledgements

Many people at BDO have helped with this book at various stages: Simon Bevan, Don Bawtree, Laura Cleave, John Dennison, Jean Lancaster and Benjamin Viney. Jeremy Newman and my former colleague Andy Watson made useful comments on early drafts. I'd also like to thank Keith Willey at London Business School and Carol Harrison of City Parochial Foundation. Al Cotton, Director of Corporate Communications at Nypro, read through and commented on the paragraphs on Nypro. I'd also like to thank Simon Michaels of BDO for allowing me the time to write much of this book, while my particular thanks go to Peter Leach for years of support and encouragement – and the permission to benefit from his particular experience with, and writings on, family businesses. Many thanks also to Andrew Franklin at Profile Books, and to Paul Forty and Simon Perry.

Wherever possible we have identified material we have used which is subject to copyright, and have sought to obtain the relevant permission. The following material is reproduced by permission of the copyright holders:

The Risk Exposure Calculator; reprinted with permission from 'How risky is your company?' by Robert L. Simons, *Harvard Business Review*, May 1999. Copyright © 1999 by Harvard Business Publishing; all rights reserved.

Quotation from *Shakespeare in Love* by Tom Stoppard (copyright © Tom Stoppard, 1999) reprinted by kind permission of A. M. Heath & Co. Ltd.

Quotation from *Reflections on Gandhi* by George Orwell (copyright George Orwell, 1949) reprinted by permission of Bill Hamilton as the Literary Executor of the Estate of the late Sonia Brownell Orwell and Secker & Warburg Ltd.

Quotation from *Life of Galileo* by Bertolt Brecht reprinted by permission of Methuen Drama, an imprint of A&C Black Publishers Ltd.

Lines from *Howards End* by E. M. Forster reprinted by permission of the Provost and Scholars of King's College, Cambridge, and The Society of Authors as the Literary Representative of the Estate of E. M. Forster.

Lines from 'The Second Coming' by W. B. Yeats reprinted by permission of Scribner, a Division of Simon & Schuster Inc, from *The Collected Works of W. B. Yeats, Volume 1: The Poems* edited by Richard J. Fineran, copyright © 1924 The Macmillan Company; copyright renewed 1952 by Bertha Georgie Yeats, all rights reserved.

Lastly I acknowledge my wife's patience with my writing most of this book either in the evenings or on holiday.

Notwithstanding all these acknowledgements, the mistakes – all of them – are my own. In a book on governance you'd hardly expect the author to say anything else.

Rupert Merson

Bibliography

Badaracco, Joseph L. (2002) *Leading Quietly*, Harvard Business School Press.

Cadbury, Adrian (2002) *Corporate Governance and Chairmanship: A Personal View*, Oxford University Press.

Clarke, Thomas (ed.) (2004) *Theories of Corporate Governance*, Routledge.

Empson, Laura (ed.) (2007) *Managing the Modern Law Firm: New Challenges, New Perspectives*, Oxford University Press.

Fama, Eugene & Jensen, Michael (1983) 'Separation of ownership and control', *Journal of Law and Economics*, Vol. 26, No. 2.

Gourevitch, Peter A. & Shinn, James (2005) *Political Power and Corporate Control: The New Global Politics of Corporate Governance*, Princeton University Press.

Leach, Peter (2007) *Family Businesses: The Essentials*, Profile Books.

Likierman, Andrew (2007) 'Measuring the success of the board', *ICAEW Finance and Management Newsletter*, March (available from the ICAEW website).

Merson, Rupert (2003) *Non-executive Directors: A Guide for Small and Medium Size Enterprises*, Profile Books.

Monks, Robert & Minow, Neil (2006) *Corporate Governance*, third edition, Blackwell.

Partnoy, Frank (2003) *Infectious Greed*, Profile Books.

Quoted Companies Alliance (2005) *Corporate Governance: QCA Guidelines for AIM Companies*, QCA.

Simons, Robert L. (1994) *Levers of Control: How Managers Use Control Systems to Drive Strategic Renewal*, Harvard Business School Press.

Smith & Williamson (ed.) (2006) *Professional Practices Handbook*, fifth edition, Tottel.

Solomon, Jill (2007) *Corporate Governance and Accountability*, second edition, Wiley.

Notes and references

1 Quoted in the *Sunday Times*, 25 May 2003.

2 Quoted in the *Daily Telegraph*, 1 February 2009.

3 Quoted in *The Economist's* obituary of Boris Fyodorov, 29 November 2008.

4 Amar Bhide (2003), 'The questions every entrepreneur must answer', *Harvard Business Review*, December.

5 www.businessdictionary.com

6 Ibid.

7 Peter F. Drucker (1954), *The Practice of Management*, 1993 edition, Collins.

8 Milton Friedman (1962), *Capitalism and Freedom*, Chicago University Press.

9 Committee on Corporate Governance, Final Report, London, 1998.

10 Reported in the *Financial Times*, 3 February 2009.

11 *Climbing out of the Credit Crunch: ACCA Policy Paper*, Association of Chartered Certified Accountants, September 2008.

12 *Financial Times*, 8 March 2009.

13 Quoted in, of all places, *The Times Literary Supplement* on 9 January 2009.

14 Reported in the *Financial Times*, 13 March 2009.

15 Quoted in *Fortune* magazine, October 2003.

16 Jill Solomon (2007), *Corporate Governance and Accountability*, second edition, Wiley.

17 Department of Trade and Industry (2002), *Social Enterprise: A Strategy for Success*, DTI.

18 Charity Commission (2007), *Trustees, Trading and Tax: How Charities May Lawfully Trade*, CC35, Charity Commission, April.

19 Richard Fletcher, *Daily Telegraph*, 18 November 2008.

20 Much of the data in this paragraph is taken from Richard Fletcher's piece in the *Daily Telegraph*.

21 J. K. Galbraith (1955), *The Great Crash: 1929*, reprinted many times since.

22 George Orwell (1949), 'Reflections on Gandhi', collected in *Shooting an Elephant*, 2009 edition, Penguin Classics.

23 Robert Simons (1995), *Levers of Control*, Harvard Business School Press.

24 *The Times*, 17 July 2003, quoted by Stuart Crainer and Desmond Dearlove in *Business Strategy Review*, autumn 2003.

25 Financial Reporting Council (2008), *The Combined Code on Corporate Governance*, June.

26 Quoted in the *Sunday Times*, 30 March 2008.

27 Quoted in *The Times*, 30 March 2008.

28 Quoted in the *Daily Telegraph*, 10 December 2008.

29 Quoted in the *Financial Times*, 19 April 2002.

30 As reported in the *Sunday Times*, 16 November 2008.

31 Reported in the *Guardian*, 7 April 2009.

32 Speech to the RSA, November 1996, reported in RSA journal Vol. CXLV, No. 5476 Jan.–Feb. 1997.

33 John Hamm (2002), 'Why entrepreneurs do not scale', *Harvard Business Review*, December.

34 24 April 2008.

35 As reported by Arthur Levitt, former Chairman of the SEC, in the *Financial Times*, November 2002.

36 Financial Reporting Council (2008), *The Combined Code on Corporate Governance*, June.

37 Aidan Berry & Lew Perren (2000), *The Role of Non-Executive Directors in United Kingdom SMEs*, Certified Accountants Educational Trust.

38 Rupert Merson (2003), *Non-executive Directors, A Guide For Small and Medium Sized Enterprises*, Profile Books.

39 Derek Higgs (2003), *Review of the Role and Effectiveness of Non-Executive Directors* ('The Higgs Report'), DTI.

40 'Can leopards change their spots?', *Accountancy*, December 2002.

41 Derek Higgs (2003), *Review of the Role and Effectiveness of Non-Executive Directors* ('The Higgs Report'), DTI.

42 Rupert Merson (2005), *Travelex: Project Olympic A*, London Business School Case Study.

43 For an interesting discussion of this in the context of negotiation see Robert Mnookin (1993), 'Why negotiations fail: An exploration of barriers to the resolution of conflict', *Ohio State Journal on Dispute Resolution*, Vol. 8, No. 2.

44 E. M. Forster (1910), *Howards End*, 2000 edition, Penguin Classics.

45 Jill Solomon (2007), *Corporate Governance and Accountability*, Wiley.

46 Quoted by Joseph Badaracco in *Defining Moments*, Harvard Business School Press (1997), from G. B. Richardson (1972), 'The organisation of industry', *Economic Journal*, Vol. 82.

47 Joseph Badaracco (1997), *Defining Moments*, Harvard Business School Press.

48 Thomas Clarke (ed.) (2004), *Theories of Corporate Governance*, Routledge.

49 Peter Gourevitch & James Shinn (2005), *Political Power and Corporate Control: The New Global Politics of Corporate Governance*, Princeton University Press.

50 Gary Hamel (2009), 'Moon shots for management', *Harvard Business Review*, February.

51 Financial Reporting Council (2008), *The Combined Code on Corporate Governance*, June.

52 As reported in the *Daily Telegraph*, 5 January 2009.

53 As reported in the *Financial Times*, 19 February 2009.

54 Referred to in *The Economist*, 17 January 2007.

55 Financial Reporting Council (2009), *Review of the Effectiveness of the Combined Code: Call for Evidence*, March.

56 Shona Brown & Kathleen Eisenhardt (1998), *Competing on the Edge*, Harvard Business School Press.

57 Robert Simons (1994), *Levers of Control: How Managers Use Control Systems to Drive Strategic Renewal*, Harvard Business School Press.

58 National Hub of Expertise in Governance (2005), *Good Governance: A Code for the Voluntary and Community Sector*, July.

59 Discussed in Charles Handy (1994), *The Empty Raincoat: Making Sense of the Future*, Hutchinson.

60 Reported in the *Daily Telegraph*, 24 July 2006.

61 Personal conversation.

62 Roger Martin (2002), *The Responsibility Virus*, Basic Books.

63 As reported in the *Independent*, 7 October 2008.

64 Discussed in the *Guardian*, 28 July 2007.

65 Alfie Kohn (2003), *Punished by Rewards*, Houghton Mifflin.

66 Quoted by Alfie Kohn in *Punished by Rewards*.

67 Financial Reporting Council (2008), *The Combined Code on Corporate Governance*, A.6.

68 Ibid.

69 Andrew Likierman (2007), 'Measuring the success of the board', *ICAEW Finance and Management Newsletter*, March (available from the ICAEW website).

70 Financial Reporting Council (2008), *The Combined Code on Corporate Governance*, A.5.

71 Financial Reporting Council (2008), *The Combined Code on Corporate Governance*, Schedule B.

72 See for example Rakesh Khurana & Nitin Nohria (2008), 'It is time to make management a true profession', *Harvard Business Review*, October.

73 Warren Bennis (1997), *Managing People Is Like Herding Cats*, Atlantic Books.

74 Kenneth Lay, CEO of Enron. Lay's speech has entered the folklore of governance writing and has been quoted everywhere from US Senate committee hearings downwards. I came across it in Robert Monks & Neil Minow (2006), *Corporate Governance*, third edition, Blackwell.

75 Reported in the *Daily Telegraph*, 7 January 2009.

76 Quoted in the records of the Committee's business for 20 March 2002.

77 Ibid.

78 Louis D. Brandeis (1914), *Other People's Money and How the Bankers Use It* – 1995 edition published by Bedford/St Martin's, and quoted in Adrian Cadbury (2002), *Corporate Governance and Chairmanship: A Personal View*, Oxford University Press.

79 PricewaterhouseCoopers.

80 Quoted in *The Economist*, 24 January 2009.

81 James Surowiecki (2004), *The Wisdom of Crowds: Why the Many Are Smarter Than the Few*, Little, Brown.

82 Michel de Montaigne, *Essays*, 1.39.

83 Renato Tagiuri & John Davis (1982), *Bivalent Attributes of the Family Firm*. Working Paper, Harvard Business School; reprinted 1996, *Family Business Review*, Vol. 9, No. 2, 199–208.

84 Stoy Hayward and the London Business School (1990), *Managing the Family Business in the UK*, BDO Stoy Hayward.

85 Cyril Parkinson (1958), *Parkinson's Law, or the Pursuit of Progress*, John Murray.

86 Abraham Zaleznik seems to be one of the earliest – *Harvard Business Review*, May 1977.

87 John Kotter (1996) uses this diagram to contrast leadership and management in *Leading Change*, Harvard Business School Press.

88 J. S. Newman (1997), 'Leadership and management', *Business Growth and Profitability*, January.

89 J. S. Newman (1997), 'Leadership and management', *Business Growth and Profitability*, January.

90 Reported in *The Economist*, 17 January 2009.

91 Robert Simons (1999), 'How risky is your company?', *Harvard Business Review*, May.

92 S. E. Finer (1997), *The History of Government*, Oxford University Press.

93 Quoted in the *Financial Times*, 19 February 2009.

94 As retold by Lehman's ex-Head of Communications to *The Times*, 14 December 2008.

95 Ibid.

96 Ibid.

97 For an excellent discussion of the 'quiet leader' see Joseph L. Badaracco (2002), *Leading Quietly*, Harvard Business School Press.

98 Frederick W. Taylor (1911), *The Principles of Scientific Management*, Harper Bros.

99 Ibid.

100 Jim Collins (2001), *Good to Great: Why Some Companies Make the Leap ... and Others Do Not*, Harper Collins.

101 Ricardo Semler (2003), *The Seven Day Weekend*, Century.

102 Rakesh Khurana (2002), 'The curse of the superstar CEO', *Harvard Business Review*, September.

103 Andrew Campbell (2003), 'How lean do you want your machine?', *Financial Times*, 14 August.

104 Harold Leavitt (2003), 'Why hierarchies thrive', *Harvard Business Review*, March.

105 Ricardo Semler (2003), *The Seven Day Weekend*, Portfolio.

106 Financial Reporting Council (2008), *Guidance on Audit Committees*, October.

107 Ibid.

108 Adrian Cadbury (2002), *Corporate Governance and Chairmanship: A Personal View*, Oxford University Press.

109 Ibid.

110 Charles Mackay (1852), *Memoirs of Extraordinary Popular Delusions and the Madness of Crowds*, 2002 edition, Metro Books.

111 Ibid.

112 James Surowiecki (2004), *The Wisdom of Crowds*, Little, Brown.

113 Gary Hamel (2009), 'Moon shots for management', *Harvard Business Review*, February.

114 Ibid.

115 Adam Smith (1759), *The Theory of Moral Sentiments*, 2002 edition, Knud Haakonssen (ed.), Cambridge University Press, p. 222.

116 Quoted in the *Financial Times*, 26 February 2009.

117 *Accountancy*, March 2009.

118 Financial Reporting Council (2008), *The Combined Code on Corporate Governance*, C.3.1.

119 John Ruskin (1862), *Unto This Last*, 2007 edition, Filiquarian Publishing.

Index